James Black Cameron

Poems and Songs

James Black Cameron

Poems and Songs

ISBN/EAN: 9783337179601

Printed in Europe, USA, Canada, Australia, Japan

Cover: Foto ©Thomas Meinert / pixelio.de

More available books at **www.hansebooks.com**

POEMS AND SONGS.

POEMS AND SONGS.

BY

JAMES BLACK CAMERON, F.E.I.S.,

GRANGEMOUTH.

WILLIAM P. NIMMO,
LONDON AND EDINBURGH.
1877.

EDINBURGH:
PRINTED BY M'FARLANE AND ERSKINE,
ST JAMES SQUARE.

PREFACE.

JAMES BLACK CAMERON, eldest son of the late John Cameron, engineer, was born in Greenock on the 6th October 1833. While still a child, his family removed to London; but on the death of his father in Jamaica they returned to Scotland, and settled in Glasgow. Up to this time his education had been carried on at home by his mother, a woman of considerable mental power. Being now ten years of age, his friends thought that the time had come when he should be sent to school. He was accordingly enrolled as a pupil in the Normal School, and for upwards of three years studied under Mr Hislop, the head-master. At the age of fourteen he was apprenticed as an engineer in the Vulcan Foundry, Port Dundas; but before six months had passed, his right arm was accidentally caught by some machinery, and so mangled that amputation of the hand was necessary. Unable now to prosecute a trade, he returned to the Normal School, and under the tuition of the head-master, Mr Forbes, now of Dumfries Academy, made such progress that at the early age of seventeen he received an appointment as assistant to the late Mr Craig, of the Glasgow Industrial Schools; and about a year thereafter he was elected teacher of Springbank School. Although prior to this he had shown a strong tendency to literature, it was at this time that its pursuit became an absorbing passion.

Conducting a large school, with little assistance, during the day, and an evening school for five nights in the week, would be considered sufficient work for any man; but the love of literature was so strong within him that his studies were often carried on till early morning. This could not continue. His health gave way. He resigned his situation, and for six months he was confined to the house. During this enforced retirement he applied himself to the study of the Spanish language, intending to go out to an uncle in South America, for the sake of his health; but his uncle dying, this design had to be abandoned. It now became a serious question what he should do; whether he should devote himself entirely to literature, or resume teaching. He accordingly wrote to Sir E. Bulwer Lytton, enclosing a specimen of his work, stating his position, and asking for advice. To this a very complimentary and kind reply was received, advising him to continue his studies, but not to abandon his profession until he had made such a name in literature as would secure him against the necessity of becoming a literary hack. Shortly afterwards he received an appointment to Hollandbush School, near Denny, where for five years he taught so successfully that very great regret was felt when he accepted his last situation, the mastership of Grangemouth Subscription School.

During all this time he was storing his mind from the treasures of Spanish ballad and Norse legend; yet he never ceased to cultivate his powers as a writer, both of prose and of poetry; and his contributions were frequent, not only to the columns of the local papers, but also to those of Edinburgh and Glasgow. Had he devoted himself entirely to literature, he would doubtless have won for himself a high position among the writers of this country. But working all day in a worrying and mind-fagging profession, his productive powers were limited; but yet he has produced some pieces which we venture to predict will live.

He died at Grangemouth on the 22d of May 1876, leaving a widow and two children.

At the urgent request of many friends this volume —a selection from his poetical compositions—has been issued.

CONTENTS.

	PAGE
EVENING HYMN,	1
FLOWER IDYLLS:	
THE WATER LILIES,	2
THE FORGET-ME-NOTS,	5
THE TULIP,	12
AN APOCALYPSIS,	16
AN ADDRESS OF WELCOME TO THOMAS BROWN, ESQ.,	28
TO A COQUETTE,	31
TO STELLA,	33
BRIDAL-CAKE DREAM,	34
THE DEAD HOPE,	36
MAGGIE, DARLING,	37
BRIGHT EYES,	38
BRIDAL SONG,	39
SAD THOUGHTS,	39

CONTENTS.

	PAGE
BIRTHDAY FANCY—	
TO ISABELLA CLARK,	41
TO MISS CLARK,	44
JANUARY 1, 1872,	50
RETHE,	52
LONG AGO,	55
SKADI'S CHOICE,	57
A CUMBERLAND LEGEND,	62
THE BRIGHT SIDE OF THINGS,	64
FANCY,	65
WHAT ODIN'S EYE BOUGHT,	67
MŒROR CORDIS,	72
IN MEMORIAM,	73
A FANCY,	75
NELLY,	78
LINES IN MEMORIAM,	79
THE STAR AND THE STREAM,	80
SONNET,	81
DEDICATED TO MISS ANNIE RUSSELL, FALKIRK—	
BIRTHS,	82
MARRIAGES,	83
DEATHS,	83
HANS CHRISTIAN ANDERSEN,	84
ABSENT FRIENDS,	85

CONTENTS.

	PAGE
MILLHALL,	88
THE OLD DEAR DAYS,	89
HASSAN'S AMULET,	92
TO MARY,	108
KEEP FRESH THE HEART,	109
THERE'S A BIRD IN BANTON,	110
THE FIRST STOWN KISS,	111
MARY O' BANKIER,	114
LINES TO THE MISSES SAMUEL,	115
TO THEE,	116
SONG,	117
SONNET,	117
SONNET,	118
ELEGY ON THE DEATH OF PETER LUCKIE, A SCHOOL COMPANION,	119
BEAUTIFUL EYES,	121
COULD I FORGET,	122
MY PROPOSED NEW PHILOSOPHY,	124
FRAGMENT,	125
VALENTINE,	125
THERE IS A STAR,	126
SONG,	128
MAN,	129
HYMN TO EROS,	130

CONTENTS.

	PAGE
LIFE AND DEATH,	133
THE FAREWELL,	134
DREAMS,	136
THE ENIGMA OF TIME,	137
NELLY,	139
WRITTEN ON THE DEATH OF MR ROBERT BUCHANAN,	139
THE RIME OF THE WICKED EARL,	141
INDEX OF FIRST LINES,	177

POEMS.

EVENING HYMN.

Evening's shades, as daylight fades,
    Mantle sadly earth and sea;
The holy hour, with solemn power,
    Bids us lift our voice to Thee.
Giver Thou of light and gloom,
Lord of life and of the tomb,
Hear us, mighty Father, aid us!
Let Thy wings of power o'ershade us!
    Keep us! guide us!
In Thy well-proven mercy hide us.
    Children of the second birth,
We are feeble, frail, unstable;
Thou alone to help art able.
Guide us, aid us, overshade us,
    As the evening shades the earth.

FLOWER IDYLLS.

NO. I.—THE WATER LILIES.

ALL noon I loitered in the sheltering wood,
    And listened to the gnat's incessant hum,
Wooing me to a dreamful, drowsy mood;
    But when the arrows of the sun were come
West-slanted, I o'erstrode the heathy slopes,
    Upward and upward, till I crossed the hill;
Then down and down, on to the hazel copse
    That borders the broad stream, and there stood still
        Beside the Water Lilies.

Out in the midstream, strong and smooth and deep,
    With an unceasing hiss in undertone,
The main mass of the water holds its sweep
    As if one thought—one earnest thought alone—
Were its;—a restless longing for the sea—
    A fierce impatience for the unknown end;

But at the edge, as gentle as can be,
   The broken currents interfuse and blend
      Among the Water Lilies.

The wooing wave crisps in around their petals,
   And dallies with their broad fronds as it goes;
And every moment languidly unsettles
   The silver water-stars' serene repose.
But on, and on, and on—for ever, ever—
   The river runs—for ever on and on—
The fresh wave comes, and fresh the sedges shiver,—
   New wooers follow, when the old are gone,
      To the white Water Lilies.

"Ah me!" I said, with misty eyes and grave,
   " I am a rootless weed that floats away,
And passes onward with the passing wave,
   Powerless to seek a haven, or to say,
I am weary, but I've found a rest—
   Here will I stay and let the waves run by—
Our labour turns to naught, 'tis surely best
   To be in quiet under the quiet sky,
      Like the white Water Lilies."

And when the moon came out, I lingered still;
   And when the stars were high I yet was there,
Dreaming sweet fancies with an unchecked will,
   And memories sadder, but not less as fair,

And not the less as dear; of vanished joys,
    And sorrows softened by the touch of time;
And in my dream the flowers took up a voice,
    And the voice shaped itself into the rhyme
        Of the white Water Lilies.

"Of perfect motion cometh perfect rest,
    And rest is the appointed end and welcome close;
We loll upon the wave, and, wave caressed—
    Lulled by the unreposing to repose—
Reck not how days may go, and come and go;
    We take the sunbeams, be they slant or steep;
At noon we sun us in the noontide glow,
    At eve we fold our petals up and sleep."
        So sang the Water Lilies.

"The wave flows on—flows on, but we are here;
    The wave flows on—flows on, but we are still;
We catch the 'wildered current in our sphere,
    And shape its wildness to our languid will.
We yield—and, yielding, rule. When waves are high
    With rain-streams from the hills, we rise with them;
And when they fail beneath the summer sky,
    With them sinks down each starry anadem
        Of the white Water Lilies.

"And if the flood comes down, roaring and red,
    Angrily tossing back its hoary mane,

We fold our leaves together, and are hid,
   Till it return to gentleness again.
So takes the meek the mastery of the stern,
   O'ercome of all—o'ercoming all at length—
Safe in its lowliness—so we discern
   That in our perfect weakness lies our strength."
      So teach the Water Lilies.

And lo! the dreamy rhythm in my soul
   Gave to my soul a dreamy sense of calm,
Cooling Hope's fever—lulling Memory's dole,
   Soothing and quiet as the evening psalm
Which breathes of labour done, and rest beneath
   Night's brooding wings, with drowsy softness lined:
So musing, I went upwards o'er the heath,
   With many a pause, and many a look behind
      At the white Water Lilies.

NO. II.—THE FORGET-ME-NOTS.

"*Sis Memor Mei.*"
Respectfully inscribed to Alexander Thomson, Esq., Ochilview.

  THE song itself is nothing:—but the name
  To which it dares to be inscribed, must claim
  Unsullied honour. Whether in the mart
  Of commerce, or when taking daily part
  In the amenities of life, his heart

Beats nobly, far removed from aught that is
Sordid, or mean, or selfish.   Therefore this
Poor essay of my muse I put beneath
The ægis of his name, that it may breathe,
In some reflected sort, the atmosphere
Of his most genial nature, warm and clear.

   Where the fernsprays bend their arches,
   Underneath the tasselled larches—
   Where the fretted ripples swerve,
   In the streamlet's sudden curve—
   Where the noonday glare of summer
     Filters through the leafy screen,
   Cooler—tenderer—welcomer—
     Toned down to a golden green—
   There, in that delicious spot,
   Met I this old friend of mine,
   Love's own token, Hope's own sign ;—
     Gold and blue Forget-me-not.

It holds up to the sun no flaunting chalice,
   With purple or with crimson streaked and starred :
And from its open golden heart there sallies
   No scent of myrrh, of cassia, or of nard.

Not tulip-like, a Cleopatra, sailing
   In pomp and glory, adown Cydnus' wave—
An Imogene it seems, forsaken, hiding
   Its tender beauty in Bellarius' cave.

No musky odour—no entrancing splendour—
    To thrill and thrall the overmastered sense;
But with a quiet and infinitely tender,
    Most graceful and most gracious influence,
Its blossoms from their humble haunts express
The gospel of a self-sufficing lowliness.

Five tiny oval petals—heavenly blue—
    Bend in a circlet round a golden eye;
And that sad legend—old, and ever new—
    Has consecrated it, for aye, to lie
Close hid and cherished in the inner deeps,
Where memory's holiest shrine her dearest treasure keeps.

    Yes! of all legends floating
        Down the River of the Years,
    No one know I worthier noting
        Than that tale of truth and tears—
    Which the teller of must say low,
        In a tone that faltereth—
    Hallowed by the double halo,
        Each divine, of Love and Death.

" By the streamlet walked the lovers, in the olden German land;
By the streamlet, where its current undermined the fretted strand;

In the tender hush of twilight, ere the bashful star of Love
Left its soft concealment by the flush of daylight's sun-beams wove.

"Downcast were the maiden's glances, timidly she looked aside,
Golden-eyed and azure-petalled, there these blossoms she espied
On a jutting bank bold-hanging: it would almost seem they knew
Danger waited on the footstep that should venture where they grew.

"Scarcely had she praised their beauty, ere the eager hand of love
Sought to seize the fatal blossoms, as they tempting hung above;
Seized them—but the treacherous footing failed him, and the river's swirl
Bore him in its eddy under, from the horror-stricken girl.

"Battling with the current bravely, battling bravely but in vain,
Love's last thought was for the loved one—Hope must part and Faith remain.

One convulsive effort made he, ere the wave its prey had got,
Flung the flowers in safety shoreward, crying, ' Love, forget me not.'

"And since then this tiny blossom, Constancy and Hope have claimed
As their own peculiar emblem, and FORGET-ME-NOT have named."

From its blue petals, from its golden centre,
   Stream subtle, viewless, but all-potent spells—
Magnetic influences, which pierce and enter
   The grey coils of the brain where Memory dwells.

The wind came freshly through the leafy shadow;
   The voice of birds came through the woodland maze;
The scent of new-mown hay came o'er the meadow—
   And o'er my heart a dream of bygone days.

Days of my boyhood by the wooded Kelvin;
   Days in the Schiftwood, where the rocks are piled
In chaos-order, steep, abrupt, and shelving;
   Days by the Gryffeside, in its dingles wild:

Days in the ancient Caledonian forest,
   Where Cadzow's crumbling castle hangs o'er Avon,
Like a hawk's nest, upon the steepest, hoarest,
   Storm-shattered cliff, above the torrents raving:

Days up in Garrel glen, with moss and heather
   Seen through the vistas of the coppice-path:
Days at the Hermitage, in rainy weather,
   When Carron Fall raised up its voice in wrath:—

All these unrolled in mental panorama,
   There, by the Millhaugh Burn, in that quiet nook;
And all the voices of life's double drama
   Were blended with the brawling of the brook.

Forget me not! The past is ever present,
   'Tis ever with us—nay, it is ourselves!
Not fugitive, and no wise evanescent—
   Not merely stored in books on History's shelves—

But throbbing, pulsing, through the veins and tissues
   (Yesterday's food is muscle of to-day),
Working in darkness to appointed issues—
   A noon evolved from out a dawning grey.

    O'er the dead so gently sleeping,
      Wherefore rear the storied stone?
    But because we would be keeping
      Back from blank Oblivion,
    For however brief a space—
      In however small a spot—
    The memory of a name and race,
      Which have been and now are not:

And whose blood, like Abel's, crying
From the dust, denies denying,
In our ears for ever sighing,
"Forget me not! Forget me not!"

Vain hope! but not without its compensation;
  If Love and Joy must share Oblivion's lot,
Yet not the less shall Grief and Desolation
  Pass into nothingness and be forgot.

"Forget us not!" should rather be *our* exclamation,
  We shall join them, but never they return.
Vainer, ah! vainer, is their aspiration
  Than ours who, many a time and often, yearn
To share their stillness and partake their rest,
  Rather than wrestle with the hollow-hearted
Schemer and schemes, whose purpose stands confessed,
Till, sick of life, we murmur, "Blest, oh, blest,
  The lot of those who lie among the Old Departed!"

"Forget me not!" ah, strong but foolish yearning!
  Outcome and end of this fond egotism of ours.
Does Earth remember at the Spring's returning
  Last year's fallen leaves—last year's departed flowers?

NO. III.—THE TULIP.

"Whited sepulchres, which indeed appear beautiful outward, but"—

Trudging along, my stick and I,
On the summer pathway, hot and dry,
Between grey hedges, all bedight
With a powder of road-dust, like a blight;—
A dirty green and a dirty white
Blended, until the aching sight,
Weary of hedgerow and weary of road,
Looked up to the pitiless, blue, and broad
Expanse of sky, with glare o'erflowed!—
And felt relief, as sometimes flows
From flying from petty griefs to those
Whose very weight of mastering woes
Deadens and numbs all meaner throes
 Under an overmastering load—
All at once a short, quick turning
Brought me, without hint or warning,
Sudden as a tropic morning,
Unforeseen by me unknowing,
Where a Tulip Bed was glowing.

With a glad surprise prevailing,
O'er the painted rustic paling
Leaned I, eager-eyed, and hailing

Beauty's very self and presence
In the shimmering iridescence.
Through the dainty lattice fretwork
(Delicate as fairy network),
Fringed round with an emerald border,
Level, with the scythe's late traces,
Burning in the sunlight's ardour—
Bowing to the wind's embraces—
Grew the Tulips, in emblazure,
Crimson, purple, golden, azure.

In the west breeze, swaying, tossing,
Bending, interlaced, and crossing,
Showing, at each shift and slope,
More tints than the kaleidoscope,
While the leaves and stems were seen
Toning in a tender green,
The ripple kept on pulsing, flushing,
    Change and motion all incessant—
Amethystine-violet blending
With the ruby's blood-red blushing—
Sapphire's vivid gleam contending
    With the opal iridescent.
Burning, gleaming, shifting, quivering—
On the emerald background shivering,
Danced the streaks—now bright—now duller—
As the wavering wealth of colour

Moved, as moves a maiden's tresses,
In the west wind's warm caresses,
When it woos them, in its ardour,
Into daintiest disorder.

With the eye to overflowing
Filled with beauty, flushed and glowing,
With the soul bedazed—entranced—
In the splendour there that glanced,
I stood gazing, with no heed on
Aught, save this small glimpse of Eden—
Till the sense's self-compulsion
Wrought a suddenest revulsion—
Till the feeling's very excess
  Dulled itself and died full-sated,
Like an appetite whose press
  Fails before a wish o'errated.
"Faugh," said I, "the illusion's gone!"
And turning set me to depart;
"O Tulip, eye-server, eye-pleaser alone,
Scentless art thou, and black in the heart."

Flaunt up, gaudy Delilah of flowers,
Daintily symbol the soul of the age—
The glitter and glare of this time of ours,
With its Mammon-worship and golden rage.
The Pharisee's shibboleth has grown stale—
"Stand aside, I am holier than thou."

Vae Victis—with gold in the other scale,
'Tis "Stand aside, I am richer"—now.
The Bible is put on the upper shelf,
The bank-book takes its place in the heart;
Men "make themselves," and worship that self,
And show rules alike in the church and the mart.

Trample the violet under foot—
It only emblems modest worth:
The pure white lilies uproot—uproot—
They merely crowd and cumber our earth:
The care of the age is not for these,
The scentless tulip-beds better please—
Tinsel and gaud, and gold and blood,
Fair-seeming lies and hypocrisies,
Sanctified sin and painted mud—
These be thy gods, O Israel, now;
Bow to them, Mammonish worldlings, bow!
But not for ever. How long, how long,
Shall we bear the rule of the gilded wrong?
Bring forth, O Asked of God, thy sword,
And hew this Agag before the Lord!

AN APOCALYPSIS.

"Verum ego non tam aliis legem ponam, quam legem vobis meæ propriæ mentis exponam: quam qui probaverit, teneat: cui non placuerit, abjeciat."
—*Petrarch, De Vita Solitaria, lib. i., tract iv., c. 4.*

CLOSER and nearer still, Annie! closer and nearer still!
See, the twilight sky grows greyer, and the twilight air grows chill,
And the fir-wood lies as black as death in the shadow of the hill.

It is the holy time of earth, and softly everywhere
The baptism of the gentle dew hallows the scented air,
And the lilies stoop their stately heads as if they bent in prayer:
Straight up above through a jagged cleft is a belt of intensest blue,
An angel's path, besprinkled with a bashful star or two;
And we are alone in the garden—alone, love—I and you.

Closer and nearer yet, Annie! closer and nearer yet!
My hair is flecked with grey, darling! yours is black as jet;
My face is somewhat sadly stern—the lines are firm and set;
While yours is fresh as a rosebud, with the dews of morning wet:
And your heart is full and joyous as the May-day song of birds;
Yet your trustful eyes have said, and your low-whispered words,
That you love me, darling—love me! though sad and worn and grey;
And the old church chimes to-morrow morn ring out our marriage-day!

Let us sit down here, Annie—here, under the bee-loved lime,
While I tell an old, old story—told for the thousandth time.

Many a day ago, Annie, by the grey, hungry sea,
There was an ivied cottage under a sycamore tree,
With a dainty-latticed porch and a quaint old pointed roof;
And I saw it—and all in it—through a veil of fairy-woof.

To idle eyes 'twas but a cottage by the old brown
    sea-strand;
But to me it was haloed with the light of the Elfin land,
For a potent witch lived in it—a lady, young and fair,
With the starlight prisoned in her eyes, and the sun-
    beams in her hair.

Why linger? we were much together (nay, darling, do
    not start);
I loved her—yes, yes, Annie! I loved her with all
    my heart!
I was faint with the thirst of love —like Moor, mirage-
    beguiled;
It was many a day long since, love! and my heart
    was foolish and wild—
Many a day long since, Annie; when you were but a child.

She was older by two summers, but her light and joy-
    ous tone
Made the years that had flown o'er her seem less than
    were my own;
For I was always somewhat sad, and though the brow
    be smooth,
The irk of thought will overveil in part the bloom of
    youth.
And we were much together; and she knew of my love,
For a thousand things can speak, though the shy lips
    will not move.

And many a nameless token seemed confirmation
    plain,
That if I dared to dream of her my dreaming was not
    vain.
Yes, love! I thought—woe's me! I thought that I
    was loved again!

Closer, darling! closer to me. What did the lady
    care,
So that her pride might be fed fat, what sorrow I
    should bear?
She played with my heart as the wind with the tangles
    of your hair;
But I lay lapped in my love-lulled sleep—in my Delilah
    dream—
Holding yesterday as naught, to-morrow of small
    esteem,
So that to-day the sky was bright, over love's summer
    stream!

But I awoke one day, darling! and it was in this
    wise—
The scene has many a time since then sprung up be-
    fore my eyes—
At the summer eventide, as wont, I went to be with
    her,
And the cottage was alive with a murmur and a
    stir:

At the door stood little Helen, the lady's blue-eyed
    sister;
We were great friends—the child and I—and, bending
    down, I kissed her.
"That's two to-day" she lisped—"one from Frank
    and one from you;
I shall be rich in kisses soon; come into the parlour
    —do.
They're all in there—Frank and them all." I passed
    into the room,
And through my heart there shot a chill, and o'er my
    eyes a gloom;
And the sunshine lost its glory, and the summer lost
    its bloom.

This was her sailor-lover—abroad for many a day.
They had been troth-plighted, Annie! before he went
    away;
Yet, with this bond upon her, the coquette's black,
    hollow heart
Could feign the blush and smile of love with a cool,
    accursed art—
Could lure the trusting soul o'er a false and fatal track,
And wake a music in my breast she ne'er could echo
    back.
And she was to be his bride, love! ere many days
    were o'er—
For it was not long at a time that he could stay ashore.

The very eve before he came, under the starlight cool,
We walked in the whispering oak-shade, and my soul of souls was full
With a passionate adoration and a fond and credulous trust;
Hope's upward-pointing wings dreamed naught of the defiling dust.
Soft-voiced was the lady and gracious. We parted with a kiss;
But not a word of the morrow's comer—never a word of this!
I sat there, marble-masked in face that not a line could swerve,
With a lazy lip-smile, and a chain upon each quivering nerve.
I bade the bridegroom welcome gay, with some faint touch of ruth—
I praised the lady's beauty—I praised her faith and truth;
I chattered with a careless scorn, and home the words were driven
In that bland tone which cannot be resented—nor forgiven;
And, to the devil in my heart, it was enjoyment rich
To catch her half-appealing look, and the quick, convulsive twitch
That writhed in the corners of her mouth—in all her will's despite.
I do regret it. Gentleness is ever truest might.

I was wont to leave them with "Good-night;" "Good-
 bye" I bade them now.
Smiling, and scoffing, and shaking hands, with an
 ice-cold, ice-smooth brow,
Forth from the disenchanted land I passed into the night,
Where the cold, broad sea lay moaning in the wan
 and ghostly light.
My heart was all benumbed, in a transient, pulseless
 sleep,
Like the crouching lion's pause ere he takes his deadly
 leap—
Voiceless and hushed, and numbed, and still, as it could
 never wake—
Still! ay, as earth is still, till the crashing thunders
 break.

The loss of accustomed wealth, and the view of present
 death,
Will cramp and load the stifled breast till it draw a
 'bated breath;
Yet still the true heart's dauntless will has power
 within itself
To front the shadowy terror, and to scorn the vanished
 pelf.
Friends part and perish, Annie! and the heart is
 stricken sore,
Yet the empty fountain fills, and the void is void no
 more;

But when faith is smote to death, and the once all-
    cloudless sky
Grows murky with the lethal gloom of the incarnate lie,
Then a vague and shapeless fear has birth, and a gnaw-
    ing doubt springs up,
And each heart's spring is made deadly by deceit's
    envenomed cup.

When earth hath lost this primal truth Heaven only can
    redeem.
I have no memory of that night save as a hideous dream
Of tossings, and groanings, and tears, and sights and
    sounds of dread,
And fierce repinings, and mad prayers that I were
    with the dead;
And a horror of the darkness and its visions of affright—
Till the day broke in sunshine, and then I cursed the
    light.
Yet though nigh wounded unto death, with many an
    aching scar,
My soul came forth victorious from the torturing
    heart-war;
For the burning love that had been my very life of life,
Was thrown in the deadly wrestle of that terrible night's
    strife,
And cast aside and spurned by the indomitable will.
But though the venomed shaft was drawn, the wound
    kept rankling still.

The waves rave out their strength and lull, and the
    mad waves rest again;
But the tall ship's thick-ribbed timbers, and her costly
    stuffs and men
No more shall find the haven, where the watchers
    watch in vain.
A chaos of chafed and shapeless shreds, it strews the
    watery way—
Like a veil of horror drawn 'twixt the sea and the con-
    scious day.

Haggard, and wan, and leaden-eyed—even of hope
    forlorn—
And hope is long and loth to leave the heart in which
    'tis born—
I left the place so woful now—an Eden but of late—
Borne up by the sustaining strength of that disdainful hate
That dares to take the doubtful odds and match itself
    with Fate.

The days went by, the weary days—a long and laggard
    train;
With little respite from my woe—small healing of my
    pain;
For I sought the healing in myself—in myself I placed
    the trust;
But vain the hope; and vain the help sought from the
    son of dust.

I found his loudliest-vaunted goods but tawdry,
  tinselled ills;
Till, from the grim valley of death, I looked up to the hills
Whence the aid cometh; and it came, and the long
  war was o'er;
Then peace fell on the vexing thoughts, and balm on
  the aching sore.

And not alone the inner life was soothed and harmonised;
But earth resumed the pristine bloom that once
  emparadised;
And a new sense of beauty, and music, and delight
Stirred through my soul, like the first breathings of the
  young spring's might;
And the rapture of happy tears could visit the long-
  stern eyes,
As they greeted the voice and view of waters, and
  fields, and skies.
In my heart upsprung the flower of love, and blossomed
  fair anew;
And a fresh hope nursed it, and baptized it with its
  holiest dew—
For, in the flush of the flower-time, darling! I met with you.

The outward grace of form and face, and your pure
  soul's dear worth,
Are blended like the promised bridal of the heavens
  and earth,

Where heaven stoops lovingly to earth and earth soars
    up to heaven.
" Have I forgiven the lady ? "
                      Yes; as I hope to be forgiven.
The perfect love that casts out fear casts out all hatred
    too.
If I bore hate to aught on earth I could not so love you.
To be most just and wisest, Heaven doth not seek alone,
But wills and works so that our souls shall be con-
    strained to own
That it *is* most just and wisest. Our path is mercy-
    strewn!
The clouds that move our peevish gall to such repin-
    ings vain
Are treasure-houses to upstore the soft and gracious
    rain;
And the chill that falls at evening, when the sultry day
    is through,
Solaces all the heat-faint earth with the softness-
    breathing dew.

Look up to the heavens, Annie! The clouds' em-
    battled host,
Where is it now? On the far verge of the horizon lost;
And the broad unwrinkled brow of the calm old
    solemn night,
With its ineffable depth, and serenity, and might,
Is softened into tenderness by the young moon's light;

And the stars smile down their blessing on the happy,
    dreaming flowers,
And brightest of all is the lover's star—be the fair
    omen ours

AN ADDRESS OF WELCOME TO THOMAS BROWN, Esq.

AND you're back to Bankier,
      Tom Brown, Tom Brown,
With your lines and your rod and such gear,
      Tom Brown.
For a trout you would fish;
Faith, we know that's the wish
That gives us your presence out here,
      Tom Brown.

Your whiskers are grown,
      Tom Brown, Tom Brown;
And you're not just so barefaced, I own,
      Tom Brown.
And your velvet skull-cap
Is still sporting its nap—
People take their nap off you alone,
      Tom Brown.

And you'll fish, and you'll fish,
>   Tom Brown, Tom Brown ;
And that luck may ensue we all wish,
>   Tom Brown;
For a struggle so hard
Sure deserves some reward.
May you never want meat in your dish,
>   Tom Brown.

But some folk we see,
>   Tom Brown, Tom Brown,
As perhaps you yourself may be,
>   Tom Brown,
And the trout which you look,
May be caught "with a hook"
With which real anglers do not agree,
>   Tom Brown.

But go in and win,
>   Tom Brown, Tom Brown ;
You're not over thin in the skin,
>   Tom Brown ;
You can stand a good rub—
I don't mean in the tub—
As long as folk keep off the tin,
>   Tom Brown.

Though a tile should be loose,
    Tom Brown, Tom Brown,
To let every one know that's no use,
    Tom Brown.
If you'd make it your plan
To look like a man,
All the world wouldn't know you're a goose,
    Tom Brown.

Since the Boards heard your prayers,
    Tom Brown, Tom Brown,
Give up your sulks and your airs,
    Tom Brown.
Think the folks that you view
Are as good just as you,
And don't laugh every time a cat stares,
    Tom Brown.

Watch your health, d'ye see,
    Tom Brown, Tom Brown;
Just think what a loss you would be,
    Tom Brown.
How the world would get on
If you should be gone
Is a question that quite staggers me,
    Tom Brown.

There's a spec, be it known,
      Tom Brown, Tom Brown,
When a profit immense could be shown,
      Tom Brown,
To buy you in a trice
At other folk's price,
And sell you again at your own,
      Tom Brown.

The men'll be glad,
      Tom Brown, Tom Brown;
A glass or two now can be had,
      Tom Brown.
You're the broth of a boy,
You like to see joy;
They'll be drinking your health like mad,
      Tom Brown.

TO A COQUETTE.

Why should I waste my heart on one
Who will not waste one thought on me;
The lamp of Love is not the sun
To give out heat unceasingly;
'Twill fail at length and cease to burn,
If it can meet with no return.

But trimmed by Hope, its gentle light
How brightly warm—how warmly tender,
Illumining our sorrow's night
With an overwhelming flush of splendour;
Till, like heaven's sunshine, it makes bright
All nature with its blessed light.

Oh, what is heaven without a star,
And what is life if love be wanting?
And what can love be if there are
No gentle hopes to ease its panting?
And what hope is there left to me
If that my love be scorned by thee?

But, oh, this chilling weight of fear
Which will not leave me, will not leave me;
And those false hopes I cherished dear,
Which flattered only to deceive me;
And then the bitter, bitter pain
Of wrenching back my heart again.

Back, back again, before too late,
With one deep struggle to be free;
But I have strength to meet my fate,
How dark soe'er that fate may be.
The keenest grief, the deepest scorn,
Is conquered when it's bravely borne.

TO STELLA.

Oh thou who shinest too fatally fair,
Brightest, and best, and only dearest,
Canst thou be moved by fondest prayer?
Hear me and pity when thou hearest—
Either learn to love like me,
Or teach me to charm like thee.

TO STELLA.

I LOOKED on a fountain
Which laughed up all brightly,
And flushed in the soft wind
That rippled it lightly;
And it smiled in the sunshine
　In dimples of gold,
But beneath—its dark waters
　Lay sullen and cold.

I look on thy fair face
When smiles on it hover,
And a warm lustre lights up
Eyes, cheeks, lips, all over;
But, ah! like the fountain,
　Amid this bright glow,
The hard heart, untouched, is
　As cold as the snow.

BRIDAL-CAKE DREAM.

PREFACE.

Miss Shaw was wed on Hogmanay,
And to Bankier were brought away
Some bits of cake to dream upon,
Of which I, J. B. C., got one.
Before I went to bed, with care
I placed it, as instructed, there,
Under the pillows buried deep,
Then tumbled in and fell asleep.

THE DREAM.

'Twas summer eve—the moon was up
   In the cloudless vault of blue,
And every flower had filled its cup
   With the soft and silvery dew;
All clear and balmy was the air
And I was in a garden fair,
Decked out in summer's gayest glory;
So fair a place I well can deem
Was never seen—even in a dream,
Nor read of in a fairy story.
I saw a light and gay alcove
With honeysuckle round it curled,
And there I sat, with her I love,
The dearest girl in all the world.

I spoke of the gentle star of eve
    With its brethren of the skies,
But the only stars I thought of then
    Were her beautiful violet eyes.
Little cared I for the lustrous sky
    With its myriad fires so fair,
When I looked into her angel face,
    For all my heaven lay *there.*

Of all the flowers in that garden close
    But one had power to please,
Neither lady lily nor queenly rose,
    But the quiet heartsease;
And she alone, of all the world,
    Could place it in my breast,
That my cares and doubts might flee away
    And my bosom be at rest.

Flame for a time may hide and smoulder,
    And love may show no sign;
But it must out—so growing bolder
    I took her little hands in mine;
Oh! how it thrilled, that gentle touch—
With accents low and trembling much,
    My tale of love I told her.

" My thoughts towards thine image move
A strong and fervid tide of love,

Resistless as a mighty river,
Yesterday—to-day—for ever.
Cares and sorrows cannot harm me,
Love, if thy soft voice but charm me.
Ah! to hear my prayer incline—
Restore not this stolen heart of mine;
Keep it still, but give me thine."

Before her answer could be spoken,
The dream had fled—the spell was broken.
How long, alas! must I now wait
Before her lips must seal my fate?

THE DEAD HOPE.

BE still! be still! though thou shouldst break,
Thou fond and foolish heart of mine;
Ache if thou must—but see thou make
      Never a sign.

Short space ago, strong-winged and rich
In fairies, came a smiling Hope,
Pinioned to reach the highest pitch
      Of heaven's cope.

But in one hour its wings were torn,
One hour its rainbow tints had fled;
At night full flushed with life, at morn
          'Twas cold and dead.

MAGGIE, DARLING.

Could the heart, when hope has perished,
    Bid remembrance also vanish;
Could love's golden dreams, long cherished,
    Pass away with what they banish;
Then might this vexed heart, forgetting
    All the mastery of love's spell,
Sigh out gently, scarce regretting,
    Maggie, darling! fare thee well!

But when hope is doomed to languish,
    Memory takes a tyrant's power,
And imparts a double anguish
    To our sorrow's saddest hour.
Be these trembling lips the token
    Of a pang no words can tell,
As I murmur now, heart broken,
    Maggie, darling! fare thee well!

Fare thee well! our paths may sever,
   But my heart must dwell with thee;
'Twould be now a vain endeavour
   Did I call it back to me;
'Tis not mine—nor would it hearken;
   Since this sorrow o'er me fell,
Day by day the shadows darken—
   Maggie, darling! fare thee well!

BRIGHT EYES.

In the solemn depths of the still night skies,
The stars—those trembling angel-eyes—
   In silence and splendour
      Glimmer aloft,
   Serenely and tender,
      With glow so soft.
But brighter and dearer,
Serener and clearer,
'Tho' only of mortal birth,
Are thy beautiful eyes—
Thy love-lit eyes—
Those dearer stars of earth.

BRIDAL SONG.

Yes! deck her out in her bridal robes,
    Twine a wreath in her raven hair,
And let her waist with a zone be braced
    Of emeralds rich and rare;
Let the diamond gleam on her snowy brow,
    Though her eyes the gems eclipse,
And rubies deck her swanlike neck—
    They are pale beside her lips.

SAD THOUGHTS.

The harvest-time is past, and the ripe sheaves
Are in the barnyard, bound with thatch and rope,
And now the green is passing from the leaves
Like the illusion from a dying hope.
No more the swallows twitter in the eaves,
Or pierce with giddy flight the skies' blue cope;
And the winds sigh about as broken-hearted,
Lamenting summer's beauty, all departed!

Yet still the earth is glorious, and the heaven
Lovely beyond all other lovelinesses;
And to the sad and silent stars is given
A sympathetic effluence, that impresses

The weary heart—all sorrow-scorched and riven,
Like the remembrance of love's first caresses,
Which haunt the soul's most secret caves for years,
And fill the heavy eyes with unsought tears.

Friends fail and hopes are shattered, and the eyes
That once made joy and sunshine in our heart
Forget their wonted welcome-glance, and ties
Once deemed indissoluble burst and part;
But these are matters for no great surprise,
'Tis but the oft-played trick of the world's art;
So let these vain regrets seek the profound
Abyss of old Oblivion.   Look around.

This world of ours, methinks, is like a cat:
So with it—that is—stroke her *with* the hair,
Then things go all serenely and quite pat,
Pussy pur-purs and holds her back quite fair—
The world proclaims you "charming," and all that;
But stroke her up the other way, and dare
Think for yourself, then comes the rub, Miss Tab gets
    brisker,
Out come the talons and up curls the whisker.

BIRTHDAY FANCY.

TO ISABELLA CLARK.

Lonely sitting—lonely sitting—
  Though 'tis long since midnight tolled,
In before me there came flitting
  Dreams and fancies manifold.
Thoughts upon the present tending,
In their whirling mixed and blending
With fond memories—sunny memories
  Of the dear, done days of old;
And upon me comes a chiming
Fit of strange fantastic rhyming,
  Whims of fancies grand and gay,
      And I weave me
      Ere they leave
  One slight, fragile wreath of rhyme,
  Welcoming the happy time
  That brings round thy natal day.

BIRTHDAY FANCY.

Round, and still round, in ceaseless course advancing,
   The seasons circle, with unwearied wing,
Gay summer into golden autumn glancing,
   And weary winter melting into spring.

      Yes! spring hath wakened earth anew,
      Bringing birthdays twenty-two;
      And your sky is still of blue—
      Not a cloud at twenty-two—
      With less of grief or sorrow, few
      Ever number twenty-two.
      So give thanks where thanks are due,
      That you're safe at twenty-two.
      Years all bright in golden hue,
      Onward stretch from twenty-two.
      Now I place before your view,
      Some remarks for twenty-two:
      Be not haughty lest you rue,
      When you're long past twenty-two.
      Think of those at Garngrew—
      They were once but twenty-two;
      So you see how people do,
      Who lose time at twenty-two.
      Folk must drink just as they brew—
      Take the hint at twenty-two.

      May the year that's a comer
      Be one long glad summer

BIRTHDAY FANCY.

Laden with blessings for thee and for thine;
    Good temper and health,
    Believe me, is wealth
That surpasses the treasures of earth's richest mine.
    All good luck attend thee,
    Good wishes I send thee,
May they have the good fortune to please—
    They are these:
    May your gowns always fit,
    May your gloves never split,
    May your tea always draw,
    May your will be a law,
    May your foot never trip,
    May your garters ne'er slip,
    May you ne'er take the huff,
    May you never talk "buff,"
    May your chimney ne'er smoke,
    May you ne'er want your joke,
    May corns spare your toes,
    May no frost bite your nose,
    May your tooth ache no more,
    May sweethearts be galore,
    May you never catch cold,
    May your heart ne'er grow old,
    May your bread ne'er be burned,
    May your milk ne'er be turned,
    And whatever comes about,
    May we never fall out.

I'll just add one more,
To make out the score,
And close this long spell
With just one remark—
May you long be a belle,
But not long Bell Clark!

BIRTHDAY FANCY.

TO MISS CLARK.

Mingling soft memories of years fled for aye
And golden hopes of happy ones in store,
Returning summer sends its first-born, May,
Young and gay, flushed with sunshine, to out-pour
Choice blessings, and to hail thee twenty-four;
Like milestones meeting the wayfarer's sight,
And these returning birthdays evermore
Reminding us of time's unpausing flight,
Keeping for ever on, alike in gloom or light.

And meet it is that Summer's darling should
Thus bring around thy birthday—thou art now
In the first flush of youthful womanhood;
The May-time of thy life—upon thy brow

BIRTHDAY FANCY.

Time's wasting finger hath not pressed yet—thou
Hast never known the deeper griefs which vary
The natural current of the soul, and bow
The loftiest hopes to dust. May each kind fairy
Shield thee from this sad knowledge all the life-long May.

    It is not wholly fable
      What these olden legends tell
    Of words which, understood aright,
    Were gifted with the hidden might
      Of magic charm and spell.
Yes; there are names, themselves most dear,
      Yet dearer from associations,
Which, when they fall upon the ear
Evoke thoughts, airy forms as clear
    As olden wizard's incantations.
    There are dreams which will fly not,
    There are hopes which will die not,
There are golden memories which will never pass away;
    There are names which, when spoken,
    Leave an impress and a token
    On the heart which must be broken
Ere their music and their magic can decay.

    Mary! Mary!
      I but name the word,
    As 'twere the waving of a fairy
      Wand—the dwellers in the past are stirred,

And, like shadows to the dreaming
Fancy, they come round me streaming,
With a rustling and a flutter,
And sad, silent eyes, which utter
More than tongue can say in its wildest vagaries.
Moving in an atmosphere
Of heart memories, calm and clear,
Come the phantoms of the Maries.

The Virgin-mother and the Magdalene,
With her who sought that her two sons should sit,
One on each hand, and the great Lord between;
And she who found that loveliness and wit
Bring but disaster—Scotland's beauteous queen,
Murdered to please a vixen's jealous fit;
And Mary Chaworth—cause of Byron's sighs—
With many more, glide in before my eyes.

Away! away! I linger not with them;
My soul is with the present and with thee;
And thy beloved name, like a rich gem,
I would set round with gentlest poesy.
And if it were not that the days are gone
When fairies walked the earth or peopled air,
I'd call each airy tribe from its own zone
To tend and guard thee with incessant care.
If they dwelt but with us
I would summon them thus:

INCANTATION SONG.

Dwellers in the viewless blast,
Over you the spell is cast,
Ye who shun the light of day
Loving more night's solemn ray,
Villa, duende, elf, and fay,
By the name which none may utter,
By the awful spell I mutter,
Hasten while you hasten may.

From the dim land of dreams—
From the palace of sleep—
From the woods and the streams—
From the coves of the deep—
From the sloping sunbeams
Where your revels ye keep,
In whose bath of hot gleams
Your fine essence ye steep—
From the clouds of the skies—
From the mists of the earth,
Whence the death-vapours rise,
And disease hath its birth—
From the marsh—from the fen—
From the dwellings of men—
I have called on you once, and I call you again.

Sprites of earth, sprites of air—
Sprites of water and fire—
Ye who love the night's gloom—ye who love the day's
　　glare—
　　　Come with a fleetness outspeeding desire,
　　　　Each and all, while you may,
　　　　Come away.

　　　To each separate gentle fairy
　　　Thus I give strict charge and order
　　　To attend this darling Mary,
　　　Evermore to help and guard her.

　　　Elves who in the cups of flowers
　　　Waste the scented summer hours,
　　　Leave forsaken bud and bloom,
　　　And in her features find a home;
　　　Ye who love the lily's cup,
　　　To her forehead clamber up,
　　　Or with circled wreathings deck
　　　The whiteness of her shapely neck;
　　　Ye who lurk in the deep bosom
　　　Of the well-veiled red-rose blossom,
　　　On her ruddy lips may seek
　　　A dwelling-place, and in her cheek
　　　When roses red and white are blending,
　　　Each for victory contending
　　　In a contest never ending.

Gentler fairy elves who lie
In the odorous secrecy
Of the blue-veined violet's eye,
In her perfumed breath from hence
Ever be your residence.

Gnomes who follow Vulcan's trade
In the mountain's deep recesses,
People henceforth every braid
Of her waving nut-brown tresses;
Forging every ringlet rare
Into fetters to ensnare,
And to keep that none deliver
Her lovers' hearts enchained for ever.

Subtler spirits of the fire,
Seek her eyes and then enkindle
The lustrous light of love's desire,
Nor let grow faint and dwindle
With the chilling touch of sorrow,
But let every new to-morrow
Light those orbs up with a finer
Lustre, rarer and diviner.
Adieu! fond fancies of the olden days;
Earth would be most melancholy
Without some touch of faith and folly.
These are the spirits that make childhood's time so gay.

If prayers have power—if fondest wishes bring
Accomplishment of their desire, thy gentle head
Shall be encircled with a happy ring
Of the most wished-for blessings earth has bred.
All gentlest thoughts shall ever light on thee,
All golden fancies of extremest scope,
And joys more dear than love—if such there be—
And softest memory and sunniest hope.
  May smiles ripple o'er
  Your face, as of yore—
  Plenty and yet more plenty
  Multiplied by four and twenty.

JANUARY 1, 1872.

RABELAIS—SMITH LOQUITUR.

On the threshold of the year,
 Look before and after:
Weigh the woe that drew the tear—
 The joy that woke the laughter.
From the altered standpoint view,
 Intermingling thorough,
Tears and smiles transformed anew,
 Transposing joy and sorrow;

Borrowing each the other's hue—
  Which was joy? which sorrow?

On the threshold of the year,
  Look before and after:
Weigh the woe will draw the tear—
  The joy will wake the laughter.
Credit neither sunny hope,
  Nor despondent warning,
In the life-kaleidoscope
  Who'll predict—ere turning—
How the prisms will shift and slope,
  Or their tints be burning.

On the threshold of the year,
  Ponder well the present:
Griefs are no enduring gear,
  Joys are evanescent;
Flood is not more sure than ebb,
  Till the skies be cloven—
Woof and warp to form the web
  Must be interwoven,
Whether shroud into the web,
  Or bridal-robe, be woven.

Day and night make up the year—
  Joy and grief its hist'ry;
Its woof a smile, its warp a tear—
  Their web life's open myst'ry.

Take that world the world presents;
    Neither hell nor heaven—
Not all Carnivals nor Lents:
    Smooth now—now uneven—
Trust the chapter of events:
    Act as to thee given.

RETHE.

The summer snow lay thick upon the hedges,
Breathing the hawthorn's essence out in musk;
The timid ash-bud, from its cloven edges,
Shot out an emerald fringe round each grey husk;
The chestnut trees were brave with creamy cones;
The light-green beechfrond foiled the last year's brown;
And from the braeface, ranged in golden zones,
The blossomed broom upon the firth looked down,
And Lily, with clasped hands and quick-drawn breath,
Paced up and down the garden-paths of Rethe.

The merle piped bravely from the birchen spray,
The blackbird carolled from the laurel bush,
The bee boomed past on its unswerving way,
And from the neighbouring glen, in ceaseless gush,

RETHE.

The hidden burn sent up its happy din;
The swallows twittered round the ivied eaves,
The wind of dawn across the firth came in,
And stirred the slumbers of the dreaming leaves—
And tossed the hair and blended with the breath
Of Lily, in the garden-paths of Rethe.

The freshness of the dawn and of the spring
Clothed with a dewy veil the earth and sky;
And tender dreams of hope were whispering
In Lily's heart, in happy sympathy;
And every now and then her steps were drawn
To a green mound that stood near, round and bold,
Whence she could see, under the sky of dawn,
The broad bright firth, in belts of blue and gold,
And wishful thoughts in wishful words found breath,
And Lily murmured on the mound of Rethe:

"Blow out, O wind, from the welcome west!
   O'er loch, and fell, and heather—
Blow out, O wind, my heart loves best,
   And bring its summer weather.
Fill out his sails who loves me best—
   Who brings my summer weather;
Come, welcome wind, from the happy west—
   You and my love, together!

"Blow out, O wind, from the golden east!
    The ship that bears my lover;
Its voyage must now have well-nigh ceased—
    O bring him quickly over!
My heart went with him, west or east,
    The weary world all over;
His faith has never failed nor ceased,
    Though far and wide a rover.

"O welcome wind, blow fair and free—
    From what point of the heaven
I know not—care not—so he be
    In safety homeward driven—
I know not—care not—east or west,
    Or north or south, if given
The favouring wind that fits him best,
    From any point of heaven."

And not long after, in the even-tide,
Sweet Lily paced the garden-paths of Rethe,
And listened, breathless, while he, by her side,
Told of the shipwreck, and the imminent death,
In the stern struggle with the wind and wave—
And the more terrible clutch of famine's grip,
Which held a lurid welcome o'er the grave—
And last, the rescue by the homebound ship—
And Lily fancied that the chill of death
Shot, with the gloaming, through the woods of Rethe.

LONG AGO.

In youth's happy El Dorado,
   In the golden long ago,
Ere grief's gloom, or sorrow's shadow,
   Darkling, dimmed life's sunny flow;
In hope's land of light and lustre,
Where each flower o'erhangs a cluster
   Of the purple grapes of love;
In the land where, self-enchanted,
Dreams take breath, and, beauty-haunted,
   We can neither look nor move
Without seeing through the far light,
   Flashed from fancy's fevered glow,
Fairer shapes than sun or starlight
   Gives our older eyes to know:—
In this happy El Dorado,
In this land without a shadow,
   Once we lived, ah! long ago,
In the far-off, misty, olden,
   Golden, misty long ago.

If at times the fair ideàl
   Of the golden long ago
Flits before the hymeneal
   Face, whose smile, as seasons flow,

Grows more womanly and tender,
Soon the nympholeptic splendour
   Fades, as fades the morning dawn,
And the rays of truth enshrine *her*
In a lustre far diviner
   Than the idol youth had drawn.
Youthful eyes grow dim and dimmer,
   But, lit up with subtler glow,
Brighter *hers* gleam forth and shimmer,
   With a light we trust and know.
So the present's loving real,
Dims and blurs the fair ideal
   That we dreamt of long ago,
In the far-off, misty, olden,
   Golden, misty long ago.

If at times a brief regretting
   Of the golden long ago
Comes upon us, weak, forgetting
   Life's more calmly ordered flow;
Then, anon, the dulled ear catches
Noise of pattering feet, and snatches
   Of our children's careless play.
Forthwith all old dreams we banish—
Forthwith all despondings vanish—
   Life is blest to us to-day.
Childish lispings and caressings
   Kindle fresh the heart's warm glow,

Showing to our eyes our blessings—
    We are happier than we know;
So dissolves our weak forgetting,
So our souls thrill, none regretting
    How we lived once, long ago,
In the far-off, misty, olden,
    Golden, misty long ago.

SKADI'S CHOICE.

FROM THE EDDAS.

Though faint and vigour-wasted from the loss
Of Idun's golden apples, high and broad
The Æsir piled the circling fence of flame
Round Asgard's bulwarks: and Thiassi's wings
Were weary with the long, now flagging flight
From furthest Jötunheim: and searing tongues
Up from the fire-belt leapt, and sour, grey smoke
Soaked through his plumage, and he fell—he fell.
The storm of flame out-tempested the rage
Of him, the stormiest of the Jötunkind.
So burnt Thiassi, on the roaring pile
That Thor and Tyr had heaped round high Asgard.

Far off, amid the rocks of Jötunheim,
Sat Skadi, carding chilly fleece of rime,
When on some wandering Vanirs' voices came
The tidings of the Jötun's fiery end.
Thiassi's daughter rose and took her arms—
Arrows of sleet, and icy-pointed spear,
And rime-fringed shield, and sword of frozen fire—
And bent her way toward the Æsirland;
Across the misty spume of many seas—
Through Svartheim's under-depths—through Nōatun—
And through the scented hollows of Alfheim,
To holy Hlidskjalf, where the Asa sat—
Odin himself—the dweller in Gladsheim.

In full Valhalla—all the Æsir round—
She made demand of vengeance; made demand
That one of all the many heroes there
Should battle with her for her father's death.
Then Bragi smiled and sung, "Fair maid and tall,
That way will surely end in bale of one,
Mayhap of both. Were it not better far
That one of this our noble Æsir band
Should wed thyself, and make a good return
Of living husband for a father dead?
That were revenge enough, methinks. Say now."
She passed an eye-glance round the circling troop.
The flaming beard and mighty limbs of Thor;
Tyr's stately strength and Hoenir's lithesome make,

SKADI'S CHOICE.

Blind Hodur, Hermod, Bragi, and Vidár—
None tempted her, until her swift regard
Fell upon Baldur, flashing like a gem.

The radiance of the sun was on his brow,
And on his cheeks and in his heavenly eyes,
And streaming from his tresses' amber lengths;
And this she settled in her heart should be
Her husband, and no other.
      It was judged,
By the Val father Odin's will, that all
Should straight betake themselves behind the screen
Of the broad-woven curtain that ran round
The wall of Baldur's hall in Breidablik;
And that beneath the tapestry's lower edge
The feet alone of each should be in view,
And by the feet should Skadi choose her man.

So done. The Jötuness passed on and on,
Once and again, along the curtain's length—
And yet again; and every time her eye
Fell on two feet, most wondrous beautiful,
Most delicately shaped; and every time
Her heart said to her, "Surely this is he;
Surely the bright-browed Baldur stands above."

And these she chose: and down the curtain fell:
And the wide hall rang to its lofty roof

With unextinguishable laugh and shout;
For on these feet stood gusty, bluff Niord,
The hearty, old, and blustering, boisterous Van.

Small love for laughing lay in Skadi's heart:
But she was held firm in the bond of choice,
And might nowise gainsay the issue. So
They wed, and bickered evermore. What home
Should hold them bred a never-done debate.
'Twas settled in some sort, that they should live
Three days in Nōatun, and in Thrymheim
Thrice three: so much to Skadi's wish
Niord bent, grumble-granting.
                                On a time,
Bound back to Nōatun, Niord broke out:
    "This abode of noise—Thrymheim—
        Wearies me. I cannot tell
    How I hate these nine days' time
        Wasted 'mid the foxes' yell.
    For the Bragarfull—a bowl
        Of half-melted rime;
    For the mead-fired lay—a howl
        Of wolves in the dreary gloaming-time."
And Skadi, bitter-hearted, made reply:
    "Wa! the wearisome wash of the waves
        Tossing across the sand—
    Wa! the sea-gulls' scream from the caves
        By Nōatun's strand!

Wa! the wing-mad Vanir race—
  Noon and night it grieves me!
Through the dreary three days' space
  Slumber ever leaves me."

No more she spake, but suddenly betook
Her way still northward—northward—till she came
Far past the utter bounds of Jötunheim,
Beyond the scent of Lyngvi's broomy isle,
On to the frosty plain of endless snow
Where lowed Audhumla, when time was not yet;
And there she lived alone, from that day forth,
A skater-huntress. And Niord—old Niord—
He of the delicate foot and gusty breath—
Kept aye to wind-swept, wave-washed Nōatun.

And, as the Saga adds, Beware—beware!
Not well-shaped foot alone, nor well-shaped form,
Nor charm of winsome face regard in man,
Or woman either—think on SKADI'S CHOICE.

A CUMBERLAND LEGEND.

UNDER the beeches of Earlswood Chase
The maiden steals bashfully on in the twilight:
Her eyes, as she nears to the old trysting-place,
Are half-veiled in the dew of a tender yet shy light;
And the red flush of evening is bright in her face,
And her dark hair is stirred by the faint breeze of
    gloaming,
While the rapturous welcome of love waits her coming,
    Under the beeches of Earlswood Chase.

Under the beeches of Earlswood Chase
Pace to and fro the fair maid and her lover:
And each glance is endowed with an undying grace,
And each vow is still new, though told over and over;
And the fond faith of youth and of love cannot trace
The shade of a dark cloud in earth or in heaven!
While the troth-piece is broken—the troth-word is given
    Under the beeches of Earlswood Chase.

Under the beeches of Earlswood Chase
The maid and her lover have met and have parted;
When out from the gloom where the boughs interlace,
The undreamed-of watcher has stealthily started,

With despair and revenge in each line of his face—
Where the sweat-furrowed brow and the chest's stifled breathing,
Betoken the strife in that heart that is seething
    Under the beeches of Earlswood Chase.

Under the beeches of Earlswood Chase
The lover hies home; in his happy love-dreaming
Enrapt and absorbed; and knows naught of the pace
Of the rival pursuer, whose dagger is gleaming
With a murderous resolve in the chequered moon rays.
One swift blow, one short shriek, and the slayer is flying
From the blood-dabbled nook where his brother is lying
    Under the beeches of Earlswood Chase.

Under the beeches of Earlswood Chase
Wearily, wearily, morrow on morrow
Glides away and is gone, without hope to efface
The blight that bows down the pale maid of Carlora
Like a storm-broken lily her beauty and grace
Lie low in the dust of a hopeless repining
For him o'er whose grave weeds and wild flowers are twining,
    Under the beeches of Earlswood Chase.

Far from the beeches of Earlswood Chase
Blood-haunted, unresting, the mad brother-slayer,
With the curse-brand of Cain on his brow and his face,
Wanders far 'neath strange skies, followed aye by the glare
Of those eyes that met his in the ghostly moon rays,
Many a day now long gone !—and will follow for ever,
Till remorse calls on death by some palm-shaded river,
  Far from the beeches of Earlswood Chase.

THE BRIGHT SIDE OF THINGS.

There are two sides to every picture,
 There are two ways to tell every tale,
And 'tis weak to give in to misfortune,
 Though often our efforts may fail.
Shall we not love the smiling of April,
 Because of the tear-drops it brings?
Oh, this earth would be Paradise nearly,
 If we'd look at the bright side of things.

The web of our life is inwoven
 With colours—some dark and some gay;
Let us sleep through the night of our sorrow,
 And awaken when joy brings the day.

Highest up on the hill 'tis the bleakest,
   And care haunts the dwelling of kings,
But our lot—if it's lowly—is sheltered ;
   Let us look at the bright side of things.

Good goes through the world masquerading,
   We know it not in its disguise,
What we take for a blank in our folly,
   May turn out, in time, the chief prize.
Then let Hope be our guide and consoler ;
   'Tis in darkness the nightingale sings ;
Christmas comes in the dead of the winter—
   Let us look at the bright side of things.

FANCY.

> "We look before and after,
> And pine for what is not."
> —Shelley's *Ode to the Skylark.*

When the wheat was as high as my daughter's head,
   Toddling by me—three years old—
I looked to the future before us, and said,
   "When a few short months shall have onward rolled,
The wheat will be tall, and its green have sped,
   Through shade and tint to the harvest gold."

From the present we look to the future's hours.
In spring we sigh for the summer's flowers—
For the summer's flowers and the autumn's fruit;
Only the voice of To-day is mute.

When the wheat was as high as my own bowed head,
  My daughter lay beneath the mould.
I looked on the past behind me, and said,
  "The wind of the autumn evening is cold—
Oh for the days ere the poppies were red,
  Before the fronds of the fern were unrolled."

From the present we turn to past's fled hours—
From the harvest's wealth, and the year's late flowers—
From the year's late flowers and the harvest's fruit;
Only the voice of To-day is mute.

WHAT ODIN'S EYE BOUGHT.

FOURTH DAY—ONSDAG.

" Not unto any—not to Odin even—
Can come the Nornir's godliest gift—To Know—
Without its fated price, inevitable,
Inexorable, unvicarious—
The price of pain and sacrifice—the loss,
Self-suffered, self-inflicted, of some good,
Great—but not greatest—whence the Greatest comes;
—So Ygg Alfader found at Mimir's Well."

From the Valhalla—from Gladsheim he passed—
And up the steeps of Asgard to Hlidskjalf—
The father Asa: and there throned himself.
O'er Æsirheim, and o'er Manheim he looked,
And through the depths of Elfland and Svartheim,
Piercing the distance with discerning eyes;
Till in grey Jötunheim he saw the growth
Of wrong or horrors, to be wrestled with,
And thrown, and beaten down, and that at once—
The waxing Jörmungand—the Fenriswolf—
And Hela, with the tint and touch of death.

Down Asgard's steps, through Asgard's golden gate,
Foot-hot he pressed him, on and ever on:
Weariless through the peopled land he passed,
Scattering about him, as he went, among
The human mortals, words and works that woke
The mystery of fire-craft, with the forge
And smitten stithy; and the lore that lures
The seed from forth the furrow once again,
Tenfold, and twenty, and an hundred fold.

So he went on and on; and now the blue
That bends above, made downward slope, and met
The blue of waters that swelled up to it.
Here one end of the tremulous bridge—Bifröst—
Finished its coloured curve. Here Mimir sat.
Here crisped the wavelets of the wondrous well.
The grey, grim guardian sat, uncaring all
Who came or went—who wished or who disdained—
And recked of naught, no time, but this—His price.
To him the Asa stoutly strided up,
And stoutly sought his draught.

                    "No small request
Is this that thou requirest, Asa Ygg:
There is great virtue in this well of mine,
But few have wit of that: and since *thou* hast,
It marks, besides, that thou hast worth, to boot.
Pay me my price, and thereon drink thy fill."

WHAT ODIN'S EYE BOUGHT.

"It cannot be a churl's bode that buys
The treasure, bitter-sweet, of Wisdom's well,"
Quoth Odin to himself; then out aloud—
"I, Asa Odin, willingly will give
In purchase my right hand."

"Nay, Asa, nay,
Your bode fails of my price. But your right eye
Will buy the draught. 'Tis meet the dearest price
Go for the dearest treasure. Like for like."

With a great sorrow Odin heard the word;
Yet, wotting that it *must* be so, he plucked
From its deep socket the blue ball of sight,
And flung it on the ground at Mimir's feet.
Of mighty breadth of brim, and deep, the horn
That, full of wondrous water, Mimir gave
To Asgard's lord, and, through the shaggy fall
That fringed his lip, it drained, until
The uttermost drop had passed the Asa's throat.

And nowise then he mourned the lacking orb;
For all, and more, of gladsome radiancy
That ever, in the many backward years,
Had passed through that right eye, now in one blaze
Flamed like a sudden-kindled beacon fire,
And flooded heart and brain with light and warmth.

The half of knowledge is the wish to know,

And all the rest will follow. This was his.
He saw that wisdom of the Midgard world
(Of Æsir, men, and elves, and Jotunkind),
Eye-won from forth the wavering slope, Hlidskjalf,
Or gathered from the Ravens twain at eve,
Was not enough to fit the Asa-lord
With full sufficiency to meet the needs
Of his allfatherhood. So on he fared—
North, in the face of frory winds, still on,
And ceased not, till earth, at its utmost verge,
Shot out a frozen peak, and then—was not.

On this did Asa Odin stretch him out,
And looked, and better looked, on Nothingness;
For three days' space his one eye viewed in vain
The emptiness of Neflheim's nebulous void—
Not seeing till use brought the wont to see—
Three days and nights—and then the mighty trunk
Of Yggdrasil, the Earth-ash, at whose root
Gnawed evermore the envious snake, Nidhogg,
Grew to his growing sight, from dark to dim,
From dim to clear: and then his eye could pierce
To where the cold, wan, homeless spectres stalked
Along the shore of corpses in Nastrond.
His perfect gaze into the gulf of gulfs,
Where roared and boiled the caldron, Hvergelmir,
Whose breath gave up a mist of nameless ills,
Reached last of all—even to Muspellheim—

And further was no vision given to Ygg.
Through all the time—all the nine nights and days—
Odin applied himself to Runes, and grew
Each day more wise, and every day more sad;
For sadness follows wisdom, shadow-like.

Uprose he and departed : strong and wise
If sad ; and went his way to Jötunheim,
To Loki's homestead. Angerbodi's brood
Met Odin's mastery then. The Jörmungand
He clutched at mightily, and tossed afar
Into the outer sea—its sudden growth
Apace brought tail to mouth ; and thus was coiled
The endless circle of the Midgard Worm :
Then Hela—pallid, pulseless, queenly-faced—
With eyes full of unutterable chill—
Was portioned, and departed to her realm
And rulership of death—Helheim :
And the wolf Fenrir for the time was tamed,
And followed Father Odin to Valhall :
And so the Three Ills of the Giantland
Owned Ygg's supremacy till Ragnarok.

For wisdom Odin sacrificed his eye :
Done nobly ! natheless he must meet the Wolf,
When the gods' twilight comes at Vegrid-fight.

MŒROR CORDIS.

Aching heart, what wouldst thou more now?
Little car'st thou what's in store now;
She is dead, and all is o'er now,
   Save the deathless memory.
As the current of the river
Back again returneth never,
So no more—no more for ever—
   Will my peace return to me.

From what fountain shall I borrow
A forgetfulness of sorrow?
Shall there ever dawn a morrow
   As the morrows dawned of old?
Loves as dear no one remembers,
Fires as fierce are now but embers,
Julys chill into Decembers,
   Lava-floods grow hard and cold.

But this heart must cease its panting,
And these dreams must cease me haunting,
Ere the sense of what is wanting
   In forgetfulness be lost.
There's a presence which will fly not,
There's a memory which will die not,
All Time's magic can supply not
   An exorcism of this ghost.

Listless now, and all **unnoting**
O'er the dead past, dreaming, doting,
Days on days run by me, floating
   Helmless on Time's weary stream;
Numbed as souls in lotus-trances,
Circled round with ghostly fancies,
Seeing but in side-long glances
   The workday world beyond this dream.

She is dead!—three words record it,
But within these words is hoarded
A world of sorrow—all unsordid—
   And within that world I live.
Evermore, from dawn to even,
Rests a shadow o'er my heaven;
Since *her* sunlight is not given,
   What light now hath earth to give?

IN MEMORIAM.

JANE, BATHIA, AND MARGARET STEEDMAN,
DROWNED IN LOCHLEVEN, 22D JANUARY 1870.

DARK memories of the captive and betrayed
Haunt thy sad waters, fair and cruel lake,
Girdling the prison-keep of old—whence eyes,
Wearied with hope deferred, have watched thy waves

Glinting their cold, clear, ripples in the sun,
To mock the captive with their cruel show
Of wind-stirred freedom; or, bound up in frost,
Offering a way his footsteps might not tread.

But, in the sorrow of to-day, we think
Little of all the far-off, olden woes
The lake has looked on.   Lured by Love's
Impulsive frenzy, sister after sister—
One, and another, and another still,
Drawn, by the bitter cry of present death,
Into the yawning jaws of death! the ice
Tempting affection's step into its grasp,
Then tossing it, remorseless, to the chill
And pitiless embrace of the cold wave.
Woe's me! lovely in life, and in their death
Still undivided.   Who can dare to trace
The agony of that lost sacrifice,
When Love, stronger than Death, essayed to save,
Alas, how vainly! when the merciless wave
Clutched triple tribute, reckless of the home
So sadly desolated?   Sympathy
May breathe consoling tones; but there is "that
Within that passeth show" when sorrow falls
With such a lethal shadow on the hearth.

"What sorrow is there like to ours?" well may
The parents murmur, in the bitterness

Of heart, and hope eclipsed. What shall we say?
What *can* we say? but wait, with folded hands,
The coming of the Comforter, whose wings,
Even now, although invisible to us,
Fan the far-spreading ether—hitherbound,
And freighted with the anodyne of Time.

A FANCY.

> " Where art thou, beloved To-morrow?
>   When young and old, and strong and weak,
> Rich and poor, through joy and sorrow,
>   Thy sweet smiles we ever seek,—
> In thy place—ah ! well-a-day !
> We find the thing we fled—To-day."
> —SHELLEY.

WEARY, weary of the sunlight,
  Weary of the stars;
Weary of life's sickening circle,
  Jealousies and jars;
Weary of the hollow-hearted
  Mockery of fools,
Strait-waistcoated in worldly shams—
  Pedants of worldly schools;

A FANCY.

To my heart I whisper, lowly,
    'Mid the dreary glooms,
Better things will come To-morrow—
    But TO-MORROW never comes.
The world wheels on its ceaseless way,
And we know nothing but TO-DAY.

Promised aid of purchased friendship,
    Hitherto delayed;
Proffered sympathy in action,
    And not simply said;
Charity that's not puffed up,
    Not Peter's, but St Paul's;
Advice not merely meant to sting
    And blister where it falls,
But with solace and a blessing
    Wheresoe'er it blooms:
These, I trow, will come To-morrow—
    But TO-MORROW never comes.
The world wheels on, through grave and gay,
And we know nothing but TO-DAY.

Better health and happier spirits,
    Heart to face the fate;
Former aims and former errors
    Lapsed, and out of date;
Visions of the silver lining
    Of the sable cloud;

New comfort of a self-content,
   Strong, if unavowed;
Freshened hope, that faint, but fairly
   In the distance looms:
These will surely come To-morrow—
   But To-MORROW never comes.
Vain to hasten or delay;
We know nothing but To-DAY.

Slander's fang shall lose its venom,
   At the charmer's charm;
Self-conceit confess its measure,
   Toadyism its harm;
Purblind bigots, past their noses
   See a shadowy world;
False pretence's flaunting banner
   Shall be dipped and furled;
The cant "I am the holier" banished
   To the Capulets' tombs:
All shall come to pass To-morrow—
   But To-MORROW never comes.
The world can vary as it it may;
We know nothing but To-day.

NELLY.

Little Nelly—chattering Nelly—
   With youth's freshest tones,
Musical as glancing streamlet
   O'er the glancing stones;
Make the spring-time promise dearer
   With the cheery noise,
Bring the promised spring-time nearer
   With your happy voice.

Little Nelly—winsome Nelly—
   My pet girl of girls;
Darling Nelly! in the sunshine
   Toss your sunny curls;
Make the summer sunshine brighter
   With your laughing eyes,
Make the summer sunshine lighter
   With their glad surprise.

Little Nelly—little Nelly—
   Shall I apprehend
How the autumn's full fruition
   Comes to perfect end?

Richer make the glowing gloaming
    With the promised fruit,
Richer make the blessing coming
    After weary suit.

Little Nelly—darling Nelly—
    Surely now I know
Why the Master called the children
    To Him, long ago.
Make the winter gloom less weary
    With caressing wiles,
Make the winter gloom less dreary
    With the light of smiles.

LINES IN MEMORIAM.

M. M‘Q. R. H., OB. NOV. 1869, ÆT. 22.

WOE follows even when the reaper Death
Gathers the full-ripe, seasoned sheaf.   But when
He puts his sickle in the green and tender corn,
Before the flush and bloom of summer comes,
A deeper desolation falls—a gloom
Unthought of—horror-filled: as when
The earth was darkened at the full height of noon

By the quick, chilling, and resistless sweep
Of an eclipse, undreamt of, unforetold—
When daylight died without a hope of dawn.
Woe for the husband, early stricken thus!
Woe for the infant-bud whose opening life,
Scarce severed from the mother-life, can turn
Never, in all the forward-stretching years,
Back to the parent stem, with childhood's clasp,
And kiss, and soft embracement, and caress!
Sorrow for so great sorrow finds no words;
A silent sympathy alone remains,
Full of mute eloquence—a voiceless balm
Of tenderest feeling. And the healer Time,
Unlike ourselves, says nothing and does much.

THE STAR AND THE STREAM.

Mirror thyself in the wave, O Star,
  Shine up from the shining stream:
Re-born in the reflex light, O Star,
  Reappear 'mid the glancing ripples bright,
    Like the deeds of the day in a dream.

Pass on through the bosky shades, O Stream,
    By the wind-stirred sedgy banks;
Foam over mimic cascades, O Stream,
Gleam in the meadows, and gloom in the glades,
    And flash where the mill-wheel clanks.

Firm fixed in the steadfast heaven, O Star,
    Yet glassed in the moving wave,
Image that steadfast faith, O Star,
Which up from the tide of sorrow and death,
    Breathes life from an open grave.

Pass on in thy restless course, O Time,
    As the ripples onward glide;
Yet mirror the heavenly light, O Time,
Let the star of faith in affliction's night
    Shine up from thy troubled tide.

SONNET.

REV. JOHN COCHRANE, OB. 19TH JAN. 1869, ÆT. 64.

After a faithful priesthood—long confessed
In all men's sight—forth from the holy place
Which feebly emblems the Shechinah's blaze,
Into the inner shrine—the Holiest—

Through the Christ-rended curtain he hath passed.
And now no more beside the dying bed
Will that kind voice be heard; no more be shed
The drops baptismal; never more be cast
Over two lives the indissoluble chain,
By him.   He rests from labour, and has souls
Given him for hire.   So ever onward rolls
Time's never-pausing chariot, in its train
Bearing the old fantastic mask of breath:
Birth, sorrow, laughter, tears and joy, and—DEATH.

DEDICATED TO MISS ANNIE RUSSELL, FALKIRK.

I. BIRTHS.

WE bind ourselves to life with wreaths of flowers;
Buds of fair promise blossom in the spring,
And childish voices visit us, and bring
Back the remembrance of our childhood's hours,
Vivid and fresh as in a morning-dream;
And little arms around our necks are twined,
And soft cheeks pressed to ours, till we grow blind
To all, save the fair promises, which seem

To gild the future, as in recompense
For sorrows past.　And surely it is wise
To look ofttimes at earth through childhood's eyes,
And feel within us its unhackneyed sense
Of credulous enjoyment, and its quick relapse
Into contentment, after life's mishaps.

II. MARRIAGES.

We bind ourselves to life with wreaths of flowers,
Odorous with love and rainbow-dyed with hope;
We consecrate a dome of amplest scope
Wherein to treasure up all that is ours—
Sweetest and dearest—and we call it home,
And in it place what fancy fondly deems
A true divinity—and yet of clay:
And well if this opinion lasts for aye,
And time serves not to disenchant our dreams.
It needs must be that cares and griefs will come,
And sorrow's cloud above our pathway lower:
Let love and trust but brighten—and behold
The darkness turned to light!　That sun has power
To flush the blackest vapour o'er with gold.

III. DEATHS.

We bind ourselves to life with wreaths of flowers,
But summer passes and the autumn comes—
The heart's-ease petals fall; the purple blooms
Fade from love's roses, and the trusted powers

Of friendship fail with the forget-me-not.
But death binds us to him. Day after day
Some cherished part of us doth pass away,
No more to be, but ne'er to be forgot!
So we die daily. So doth death become
Not grim and stern, but a most kindly host,
And his dim, silent land our wished-for home,
Where dwell our dearest ones—not lost—not lost—
But only waiting till this dream be o'er,
To meet and greet us on the tranquil shore!

HANS CHRISTIAN ANDERSEN.

BORN 2D APRIL 1805; DIED 4TH AUGUST 1875.

THREESCORE and ten, and then he passed from us—
Child all his life, and therefore worthiest
To move into the presence of the Lord,
Who called the children to Him. Through the range
Of all Teutonia's households—through the world
Of English-speaking childhood—falls a gloom
As the sad words are lightninged through the wire—
"The darling story-teller—he is dead."

What cares the youngster's heart for king or priest?
"Our king," it says, "our priest has passed away.

The voice that woke in Odense to teach
The elders what a wisdom underlies
Our foolishness, and piece our lisping speech
Into coherency, is hushed, and we
Sorrow, childwise, for our interpreter,
Who told our stories in our very words,
With glimpses of a world we only dreamt.
And we are left to dream our dreams, and keep
Our meanings to ourselves, like chirp of birds."

O children! well for you that have the power
To strain off sorrow through the sluice of tears;
But for the elders—woe is them! who dares
To take the passionate budding soul into
The vexed experience of the full-grown man,
And now educe the perfect harmony
That binds the infant to the grandsire's heart?

ABSENT FRIENDS.

(SONG.)

Though the rolling of rivers
  And seas may divide
The friends who once dwelt
  With ourselves, side by side;

Though we think not of seeing
    Or meeting them more,
Let their memory be fresh
    In our hearts, as of yore!

Let us think of them kindly,
    Since they have gone forth;
Their failings went with them—
    They've left but their worth:
To their faults distance lends
    A more softening tone,
And memory shall cherish
    Their virtues alone.

May they think of us kindly,
    As we do of them,
And their love make us stronger
    Life's torrent to stem;
Thus, though seas roll between us,
    And mountains may part,
In the strength of this love
    We're together in heart.

Let us think of *all* kindly—
    The burden of hate
Will bear down stronger shoulders
    Than ours with its weight;

But kind thoughts are as seeds
  Which, when scattered abroad,
Will spring up and make brighter
  Life's wearisome road.

Here's goodwill and a blessing
  On every friend's head,
With a cheer for the living—
  A sigh for the dead,
Whose memory yet lingers,
  Though they've fallen asleep—
As roses, though withered,
  Their fragrance still keep.

Let their names be to us
  As a magical charm,
Making eyes kindle brighter,
  And cheeks glow more warm.
Let us drink to them all,
  Whatsoe'er be their lot—
Old friends, ay, and new friends,
  May they ne'er be forgot!

MILLHALL.

L'Espoir, et encore l'Espoir, et Toujours *l'Espoir.*

O BREEZE of the autumn woods!
Stirring and strewing down the leaves,
Move through the glen's dank solitudes,
    Where all the frondage grieves
For the hushed voice of birds, and insects' hum,
And whisper gently in its dying ear
The promised greenness of another year;
Nor be to me inaudible or dumb,
But bring the solace from thy far-off home
    Of far-off hopes brought near;
And breathe thy freshness on my brow, and come
Recalling tones forgot not—dead but dear.

O leaves of the autumn woods!
Bright with the beauty of decay,
Flushed with the loveliness that broods
    In clouds when closes day:
Now death bedecks you with a seemly pall,
Changing, with Midas-touch, the green to gold,
And brown, and crimson, and sub-hues untold;
Fall round me softly, as the dead hopes fall

When life's year shivers in its autumn-chill;
    To death defiance fling—
"We still shall overcome, shall conquer still,
And mock thee with the moving breath of spring."

O hope of the autumn woods!
Woe, if we recognise thee not!
Woe, if in life's most harassed moods
    Thy solace be forgot!
They die not, they but make anew their life,
Of loftier woodage, spreading broader arms,
Strong with the strength to strive with greater harms,
Of sterner power to win in sterner strife.
The lesson of the falling leaves is tale
    Of hope and blessing both:
We see death life when viewed behind the veil,
And every season but a step in growth.

THE OLD DEAR DAYS.

    Here's the prattle of the burn
      As it seeks the Clyde,
    Here's the waving of the fern
      Where the harebells hide;

And the chequered sunshine flickers
    In the lownie den,
And the lynn's summer under-song
    Fills the birchy glen,
And my footsteps wander now
    Through the old wood-ways,
But they want the golden glamour
    Of the Old Dear Days.

Through the summer meadows,
    As of yore, I bound;
The laverock overhangs me
    In its heaven of sound,
Pulsing through the tissues
    Of ear, and heart, and brain,
Till its rapture languishes
    With the overstrain;
Once I could interpret
    The secret of its phrase,
But it's lost the mystic meaning
    Of the Old Dear Days.

There's the stillness now within me
    Of a stern content,
When, after passion's carnival,
    The soul keeps Lent;

THE OLD DEAR DAYS.

Rest comes welcome—welcome—
  After irk and toil,
Blest above the blessing
  Of corn, and wine, and oil:
Rest comes welcome—welcome—
  After long delays,
But this is not what I dreamt of
  In the Old Dear Days.

Cherished faces are around me,
  Love-illumed and dear;
Childish laughter comes to greet me,
  Idly musing here.
Better thus it is, I murmur
  To my carping soul;
Wherefore stir the depths where past years'
  Dateless billows roll?
But, like Rachel o'er her children,
  Still the heart delays,
O'er the dead, and therefore dearest,
  Old Dear Days.

HASSAN'S AMULET.

FYTTE THE FIRST.

In the reign of the Magnificent,
Twin Brother of the Sun and Moon on High,
The Most Serene and Thrice Beneficent
Caliph Haroun Alrashid Almyeye—
    In the fair city of Bagdad
Lived Hassan Abon Zellah,
A sort of lazy, philosophic fellow,
Who never thought it worth his while to sigh, or be sad;
Although to fortune he was more indebted
    For kicks than coppers;
He took whatever fell from luck's mill-hoppers,
    And never fretted.
And though *sans* riches, never sought to scout them,
But simply cracked his joke—and did without them.
This was his easy creed—for all that we know,
Half stolen from Epicurus, half from Zeno.

The Caliph lately, being impecunious,
Had confiscated the possessions, which
Were the just patrimony of Ben Zunios,
An Emir grown suspected (*id est* rich),
    And for that reason
      Guilty (or ought to be) of treason.
And to make sure he never should want bread
After, or through, this bit of legislation,
The Caliph, with extreme consideration,
      Took too—his head.

But somehow, it so happened after this,
From indigestion or remorse, we do not know,
His Highness found himself somewhat amiss,
His appetite impaired, his spirits low;
Tried piety and pleasure, both no go;
Consulted his physicians—and got worse,
At which he grew incensed; as who would not?
And, with a vigorous imperial curse,
      Bowstrung the lot.

    In short, the case grew such,
      That, through Bagdad,
The folk began to nod and shrug their shoulders
(First looking round to see who were beholders).
The Imaums said his conscience must be bad,
The courtiers thought it was his temper rather
—Your courtiers don't believe in conscience much—
And grew as white as any barber's lather,

And trembled as if in an ague fit;
   And now and then among them there would be
   A solemn shaking heads, as if to see
That *these* were on their shoulders safe—as yet.

  During this time, Caliph Haroun was thinking,
     As frequently sick people do,
     That, in his former life, a screw
      Might have been loose—perhaps even two,
        Or three, or more;
       And when upon this score
       There was no blinking
         The ugly fact,
His having grabbed the innocent Ben Zunios' pelf
Was not a thing of which historians would boast;
Viewed leniently, that is, even by himself,
It must, at once, be owned a most
         Ungentlemanly act.

    So, in this mood, he did determine
        To put down,
   Strictly, all tarry-fingered vermin;
   To make this first of his opinions,
   And to allow in his dominions
   Nor robbery, nor swindling, nor prigging,
   Embezzlement, nor fraud, nor market-rigging,
   Nor larceny, nor defalcations—
   In short, no sort of peculations,

Save and except the Rights and Customs of the Crown.
   So through the town
  In every quarter criers went repeating
    THIS PROCLAMATION:
"To all our subjects—dwellers in Bagdad—
To each and all and sundry—good or bad—
From the Commander of the Faithful—Greeting:
  Whoso is found convicted of the fact
  Of stealing, or of even having tried it,
  Shall suffer the full penalty of this Act,
    Therefor provided:
INTITULED—THEFT: AN ACT FOR ITS REPRESSION.
  The bowstring and the Tigris—doom and tomb—
    Without the room
  Of an appeal to any Court of Session—
  And to the Caliph every sequin of possession.
  And that the noble quality of justice
  With mercy tempered properly may be,
    Hereby we make decree
  To be observed by every officer and bailiff
  (As witness Mahomet, in whom our trust is);
  All those who are not found out *shall go free.*
    God save the Caliph."

FYTTE THE SECOND.

But Abon Zellah must not be forgot.
A porter was his trade, and he did ply it

Industriously enough; sometimes his lot
Was to be brisk, and sometimes not,
And by that circumstance was ruled his diet.

Well—like some places nearer hand,
      In Bagdad
      Trade grew bad,
And Hassan soon reached a condition
      Of inanition,
Sharper than fortune fated him to stand
      Ever before.
Of the finest sauce he'd oppressive store—
      As all have heard say,
      Hunger's the finest, far and away—
But then he had nothing whereupon to try it.

One day it so happened (unlucky day!)
That, wandering about, he took his way
Through a path which led by a garden wall.
The wall was low, and Hassan was tall;
Flowers and fruits, he saw them all.
His mouth was watering, his eyes were fixed
On the tempting fruit—what happened next?
Hunger urged; he was bound to obey;
    One leap, and he stood under
The bending trees, and began to convey
Their luscious burden, gullet-way,
Promising well and with scant delay,

His long-neglected stomach to stay.
He bolted and guzzled, and felt as gay
As a linnet perched on a hawthorn spray,
Or a lark, new-woke, when the sky grows grey
With the half-veiled light of the coming day,
Or an urchin, fresh from school, at play;
But ere " Jack Robinson " you could say,
    A voice in tones of thunder,
No " By your leave " or " Beg your pardon,"
    But " You blackguard thief "—
    Hassan shook like a leaf—
" What do you want in my garden ? "

Hassan stated the facts of the case as you
Have read them—but it wouldn't do ;
    In fact, it's a difficult job,
Persuading a man in a red-hot passion,
When caught in his garden in such a fashion,
    That you didn't come there to rob.
In that position you don't feel cool
    Enough to argue the question;
And arguments given with a mouth half full
    Of his finest fruit, the while you plead,
    Can only succeed
In stultifying the best one.

So off to the Cadi poor Hassan was hauled,
Who decided, as clearly as any Bell,
    That the action fell

To be judged in terms of the new-made law;
And Hassan was quite appalled
  When he saw
The Nubian executioner draw
Out of his vest, with his sooty paw,
A bowstring thin, and lithe, and tough.
Thought Hassan Abon Zellah,
"A little of that goes far enough
To satisfy a fellow;
This surely is coming the sentiment strong
By rather a trifle, and can't last long.
  I'm a gone gander
  If this goes on."
Then aloud: "O Cadi, I make appeal
To the fountain of justice, never shallow,
To the Most Serene and Sublime Commander
Of all the Faithful, who sits on the throne
To judge aright, in the name of Allah!"

Thus adjured, the Cadi, perforce,
Allowed appeal, with a very bad grace;
The gardener, who had growled himself hoarse,
Grew still more red about the face:
  And so they took their course
To the royal hall of justice, where
Each second day, after morning prayer,
Till noon was past, the Caliph sat
Cross-legged on an Indian mat

Bordered with gold, and the sacred green
Daintily arabesqued between,
> Dispensing justice and grace
> After his view of it,
Somewhat according to the *law* of the case,
> With a due regard to the *Prophet*.

FYTTE THE THIRD.

Humbly salaaming before his Highness,
The Cadi, with proper legal dryness,
Proceeded to lay before the Court
A duly muddled, verbose report
> Of the *where*, and the *when*, and the *how*,
Of Abon Hassan's heinous apple-stealing;
His judgment thereanent with care revealing,
> And the confounded row
Kicked up by Hassan thereupon, and his appeal-
> ing;
> Concluding with a flowery panegyric
Upon the Caliph's wisdom and benignity;
A panegyric which, for breadth and height,
For loyal depth and fervid might,
> Deserved the dignity
Of being chanted in a glowing lyric:
At least (if such a trifle we may mention)
It richly merited a handsome pension.

"Slave," quoth the Caliph, and therewith did fasten
   Upon poor Hassan
A most uncomfortable look—"You have appealed
To us, who sit here, holding both the shield
And sword of justice; what is there to plead
   That your misdeed
Should not be punished with law's utmost vigour?"
   (He meant *rigour*.
   Mais entre nous,
In law there's small distinction 'twixt the two.)
"We're ready now to hear your exculpation.
It's not for nothing we are named Al Raschid;
What have you in extenuation?
As for this robbing, we're resolved to squash it.
Our edict thereanent no one shall shirk;
As you must shortly find to your expense;
This law shall not be laid upon the shelf.
   Why don't you work
And trust to Allah? Providence
   Helps him who helps himself."

With all humility responded Hassan, mute
Till now: "O Caliph; even so—the fruit
Was there, and as the gardener testifies, I *did*
   Considerably help myself.
And now, I plead, it's Providence's turn
   Some help to lend."
At this equivocation justly stern,

The Caliph made a sign
   The case to end,
By the well-merited, condign
Penalty of the law.   'Twas *die* and learn.

   Two mutes stood out,
And in a twinkling slipped about
Poor Hassan's neck, with well-accustomed skill,
   The fatal cord.
" I bow," said Hassan, " to the Caliph's will.
He is commander whose hand holds the sword.

"According to the Prophet's holy word,
As given in Alkoran divine,
Three times to Mecca's sacred shrine
My father made his pilgrimage;
Thrice he the Hadji's garment wore,
Thrice mingled with the host of them
Who drunk the waters of Zemzem,
Thrice made the circlings, three and four,
   Thrice kissed the Kaaba stone :
Returning from the third, when age
Its crushing weight had on him thrown,
He brought with him this flake of jet,
A prized and precious amulet;
For whoso wears it may defy
The dangers of the earth and sky;

The poisoned cup, the canjiar's blade,
To him is all innocuous made.
The moon of wealth, the sun of power,
The stars of all delight, shall shower
Their influence through life's every hour
On him who owns this charm of might.
But only if in Allah's sight
The temple of his heart be white!
And every jinn and deey and ghoul
Shall hold the mastery of his soul,
If fraud, and wrong, and crime, and sin,
From him a welcome meet therein.
Useless to me the gem has been
From actions vile and thoughts unclean;
Nay, rather say, than useless worse—
It bore the predetermined curse
That waits on mortal who shall dare
To own the amulet as heir
While evil makes his heart its lair.
'Tis all, O Caliph, that can be
Called mine, and therefore falls to thee
According to thine own decree.
By the black Kaaba's kissings three,
By all the blessings of Zemzem,
By all the fringes that may be
Upon the Prophet's mantle's hem,
I call on Allah to attest
The valid truth of this bequest.

As thou art just, and justly named,
As thou art pure and unashamed,
As thou art lifted far aloof
From guile's deceit and fraud's reproof,
As thou can'st never in thy heart
Be wounded by remorse's dart;
With all its gifts of grace and power,
With all the charms within its dower,
The precious amulet is thine—
The bowstring and the Tigris mine!"

With airy, Oriental, exquisite politeness,
To Caliph Haroun's magnanimity and splendour,
Hassan made reverential tender
Of what seemed but a bit of polished coal.
Of all the powers of bad and good—of darkness, brightness,
Claimed for it, we've no doubt it held the whole,
Though in a fit of most uncommon tightness.

The Caliph's conscience whispered, "Have a care;
The look-out will be deeply, darkly blue
      For you,
If half of what this fellow says is true;
You'd better shirk the thing, and with an air
    Of royal, generous benignity
Walk quietly, tiptoe, clear out of the snare,
    With grace and dignity."

Haroun turned calmly to the right, where, near
Stood Giafar (afterwards Lord Burleigh)—Grand
    Vizier—
"Take thou the gem, for long and trusty service."
But Giafar, with a gesture brief and nervous,
With mingled haste and horror shoved aside
The precious charm, and reverently replied:
"Dread Caliph, I'd much rather not—much rather;
I promised on his death-bed to my father
(He died, so please your Mightiness, last spring)
Never to—to—take (hem) a—a—anything.
Here's Mesrour, under no such sort of promise,
Give it to him."
        The fact, though true, yet *rum* is,
He didn't see the beauty of the view;
In fact the nigger turned in tint a dirty blue,
And stuttered, "Gorra, massa, dat won't do."

The General Commandant of the Forces
Rejected Hassan's amulet with curses.
Be doomed to own that talisman accurst!
Never to plunder! never "go the burst!"
He'd put the case in this way, if he durst;
The Caliph's orders, for a single day,
Could not, by any chance, be carried out
If his (the General's) hands, in such a way
Were fettered up and circumscribed about.

Such an idea—always wishing to be civil—
Showed that the service, sir, was going to the devil!
Rather than carry that coal he'd be—bowstrung first.

The Chief Imaum (a foreigner) was sent for,
The thing, its conditions and powers, made explicit;
He listened to the terms, and promptly went for
Decided refusal, and "*no sing to do vis it.*"

The loudest howler in the Dervish College
Was offered it. He said, "Perhaps it may
Prove valuable to those who've got the knowledge
To understand it properly, I daresay;
But as for us—*it doesn't lie our way.*"

Some merchants from the Khan—a goodly row—
Were brought in and communicated with.
The gift and terms were argued *con* and *pro;*
And then the principal (his name was Smith)
Hemmed thrice, coughed twice, and made a false start
    once.
And then, for self and partners, gave response:
" If this here talisman (ahem) were made
Over us in business and in trade,
    In two short summers
'Twould *totally destroy the tone of commerce.*"

'Twas passing strange that nobody—not *any* body—
Would make a bid, but shirked it in the lump;
They shrank from it, as shrinks a suit of shoddy
After the ordeal of a thunderplump
(Copyright *that*—all rights reserved).

'Twas passing strange, none could be nerved
To make the powerful charm his own,
Whene'er its penalties were known.
Was it conscience? or was it humility
Wrought this self-denying ability?
No time to guess—but, note this, lastly,
It tickled the Caliph's fancy vastly.
He grinned serenely on all around,
And they bent them to the very ground;
Then he put on his royalest air and grace,
And thus dismissed the Court and case:

"It seems to me the fact, friend Hassan,
That no one here's inclined to fasten
Tighter about him honesty's band
Than due conventionalisms demand.
Since none, then, present, will or can
Accept your father's talisman,
With all its penalties annexed,
But backs out on some slim pretext,
You must retain the jetty wonder,
And be forgiven your apple plunder;

And, since your love for fruit is large,
We place our orchards in your charge,
With title of Head Gardener Regal,
And then your pilferings will be legal."

MORAL : Quite plain, and without a doubt—
All men are honest—who're not found out.

TO MARY.

WHAT a pettish little fairy
Is our pretty little Mary!
And how charmingly she'll pout
If she's put a bit about.
And her bright eyes brighter glitter,
And her rosy lips grow bitter;
   And the maid,
If you dare to contradict her,
Becomes a silent picture
Of delightful indignation;
On the chair she takes her station,
And she reads—reads—reads—
And pretends she never heeds
   What is said.

Ah, Mary! I regret
Having angered you—but yet

So pretty is the indignation,
   And so charming the disdain,
That I'm under strong temptation
   To anger you again.

KEEP FRESH THE HEART.

ALTHOUGH we seek in sunny eyes
   Love's light, and find it not;
Although by friends 'neath far-off skies,
The thoughts of whom we fondly prize,
   Our memory be forgot;
Though frowning fate should only bring us
Griefs to sadden, slights to sting us,
   Love unrequited, friends unkind,
Let's quaff afresh of hope's wine-cup,
'Twill ne'er till death be all dried up;
   Time will assuage the smart.
Hold evermore this rule in mind—
   Keep fresh the heart!

Gird it not round with the icy cloak
   Of cold contempt, disdain, or pride;
For, as the ivy encircles the oak
   Till all the giant's sap be dried,

So, if around our hearts we bind
    These shrouds, all life and joys depart.
Be wise; this maxim hold in mind—
    Keep fresh the heart!

THERE'S A BIRD IN BANTON.

(SONG.)

They deave me wi' clavers
    O' that ane and this,
And think ilka lassie
    My fancy maun strike;
But guesses o' that kind
    Aft turn oot amiss;
My heart was my ain,
    And I've gein't whare I like.
I dinna misdoot but they're frank,
    And they're kind o't,
And some o' them braw;
    But I carena a rush—
Just tak' this as true,
    If ye will hae my mind o't,
There's a bird in Banton
    That's worth twa in the bush.

I've walked on the sea-shore,
   I've strayed on the hill,
I've strolled through the green wood
   When summer was braw;
And the thochts o' thae auld scenes
   Are cherished, but still
I ken o' ane dearer
   To memory than a'.
It's up by Tamrawr,
   And across by the meadows;
I could gang the hail length o't
   Blindfold at a push;
But hope's just a Will-o'-the-wisp
   To mislead us.
There's a bird in Banton
   That's worth twa in the bush.

THE FIRST STOWN KISS.

(SONG.)

The memories o' the aulden days,
   Hae a magic strangely saft,
And fancy to the silent past
   Flies mony a time and aft.

But 'mang the happy thochts there's ane
   Owertaps them a' in bliss,
Kept warm in memory's cosiest neuk—
   The first stown kiss.
      Let auld Time come or let him gang,
        He canna tine us this,
      Nor a' his winters chill the glow
        O' the first stown kiss.

What rapture fa's on youthfu' hearts,
   Like summer's gentlest rain,
When the wee bit rosebud o' a mouth
   Is prest against oor ain.
She half draws back, wi' face on fire,
   As if 'twere done amiss;
But mony a thing'll be waur ta'en
   Than that first stown kiss.
      Let auld Time come or let him gang,
        He canna tine us this,
      Nor a' his winters chill the glow
        O' the first stown kiss.

Oh, years row on, and cares come thick,
   And wrinkles seam the broo,
And the lichtest joy o' early days,
   Wad buy the brichtest noo.

But aye within our heart o' hearts,
   Ilk memory o' bliss
Is faint and feeble by the side
   O' the first stown kiss.
      Let auld Time come or let him gang,
        He canna tine us this,
      Nor a' his winters chill the glow
        O' the first stown kiss.

It gars an auld man's breath come thick,
   And a moistness cloud his een,
When he dreams i' the muckle arm-chair
   O' the days that he has seen.
But o' a' the thochts o' the far-off time
   Nane dirl his heart like this,
When his wifey's maiden lips he reft
   O' the first stown kiss.
      Let auld Time come or let him gang,
        He canna tine us this,
      Nor a' his winters chill the glow
        O' the first stown kiss.

MARY O' BANKIER.

(SONG.)

AIR—"*O' a' the Airts.*"

Doon by whare rashy Bonny rins—
  I lo'e it for her sake—
There lives my love—my dream by night,
  My idol when awake.
And lang as Bonny's waters row
  In ripples bright and clear,
Sae lang my love will cling to her,
  Sweet Mary o' Bankier!

E'en as the dove afar set free
  To seek her distant nest,
So every fancy flies to her,
  Wi' her alane to rest.
There's mony rare, there's mony fair,
  But she alane is dear.
Heaven's blessing on her winsome face,
  Sweet Mary o' Bankier!

And yet it's no her winsome face,
  Though fairer few there be;
Nor yet her form's light, airy grace
  That wiled my heart frae me;

But, warm and true, a noble heart
   Shines through her een sae clear;
Gi'e me that heart, I'd laugh at fate,
   Sweet Mary o' Bankier!

LINES TO THE MISSES SAMUEL.

You came with the sunshine,
   You go with the rain,
And the meeting brought joy,
   And the parting brings pain.
This rule the world's wisdom
   Must ever obey—
"Let the sunshine depart,
   And our friends drop away."

'Tis thus with all bright things
   And dear things on earth;
Night closes our daylight,
   And sorrow our mirth.
And we sigh as each short-lived
   Delight disappears;
"It came in all smiling,
   And went out in tears."

TO THEE.
(SONG.)

Winter comes, and winds are wandering
Wildly o'er the dreary earth,
Singing with their gusty voices
Autumn's death and winter's birth.
What care I? the blustering winds
And the noise of pattering rains
Cannot move me whilst the music
Of thy softest voice remains.

Winter comes, and snows are falling,
Now the frost king rules the plain,
And hath bound the streams and waters
In his silent silvery chain.
What care I? the chilling cold
And the nipping winter wind
Cannot move me, if thy welcome,
When we meet, be warm and kind.

Winter comes, and skies are scowling,
Earth is sad and sorrowful;
Birds are silent, trees are leafless,
And the air is dark and dull.
What care I? all nature's frowning,
Sunless skies, and cheerless plains,
Bring no gloom or sorrow, while
The sunshine of thy smile remains.

SONG.

Seize, oh seize with nimble fingers
    The passing hours,
And with light wreaths of flowers
Bind the brightest, whilst it lingers,
    Whilst we call it ours!

Bathe, oh bathe its glowing pinions
    In bubbling wine;
Even while we speak 'tis fled
To the sombre past's dominions,
    With its brethren dead!

SONNET.

There only are two things on which the eye
May gaze for ever, and not know the blight
Of languid, listless, dull satiety,
Which cankers in the core of each delight,
And casts a ghastly film athwart our sight;
Changing light laughter into heavy sigh,
Until our very souls are dead before we die.

But this fell fiend, whose far o'erarching wing
Distils a venom-rain, which doth besmutch
With foul impurity the heart's wellsprings
Of happiness (or what might yet be such,
Had they free current and the sunshine's touch),
Over these twain to it is no power given—
The changing face of the beloved and the wide
    vault of heaven.

SONNET.

Many a time, ay, many a time, and oft,
A golden dream has flushed before my eyes,
Glowing with all the hues of paradise,
Glowing with love's own lustre, pure and soft,
In the still night, a fair, fond, phantom-face;
Even as the dawn dies into perfect day,
So that fair phantom-face hath passed away
Into the sweet reality, yet I can trace
Numberless dear remembrances, and see
Clearly, through all the mists of bygone years,
Love luring me through darkness on to thee;
And now that visionary face endears
Infinitely the more, since I have known
Rapture in finding that it was thine own.

ELEGY ON THE DEATH OF PETER LUCKIE, A SCHOOL COMPANION.

Was he not wise, that ancient sage,
In Greece's happier days who sung:
"They who the Father's love engage,
   Are blest in dying young?"
The scorn, the anguish, and the strife,
The sickened heart, the careworn brow,
The hopes in disappointment rife,
That lure our footsteps on through life,
   It is not *theirs* to know.
With thoughts like these I sought to quell
The sadness on my soul that fell,
   When first I learned his death;
But vainly preached philosophy;
I could not stifle down the sigh,
Nor stanch the moistening of the eye,
   Nor calm the troubled breath.
The young, the beautiful, the loved, hath perished,
Like some fair bud an early spring hath cherished,
Nipped by a lingering winter-blast!
Ah! well do I remember him.
My heart is full, my eyes are dim
   With phantoms of the past,

For memory, like a potent witch,
    By strongest incantations,
Calls up again my school-days, rich
    In dear associations.
Ah! many a loved, but now lost form
Glides in before my sight,
When the boyish heart throbbed quick and warm,
And the boyish eye was bright;
And he, the lost one, 'mid the rest,
By all beloved, by all caressed,
To share our pastime prest the game or lightsome
    jest.
Alas! the lapse 'twixt *then* and *now!*
    What thoughts in these words lie,
No more shall sorrow cloud his brow,
    Nor mirth light up his eye.
Alas! alas! but what availeth grief
        On our part?
Much! for it brings a chastening relief
        To the heart.
Mourn him; but not with such vain sorrow
As they who mourn of hope forsaken;
He hath but gone before, and we to-morrow
The same path may have taken.
Weep for him—loved of many! tears bring calming
To the heart writhing 'neath affliction's sway;
Each honey-drop that falleth is embalming
His memory in our hearts, never to pass away.

BEAUTIFUL EYES.

(SONG.)

Beautiful eyes, that swim and dance
In your liquid radiance,
Ever be lit up with joy and mirth,
Laughing and glancing starry stars of earth.
Beautiful eyes, violet eyes,
Shine on one softly, beautiful eyes!

Deep in the soul's most secret cells,
The spirit of love in silence dwells;
But his presence we see in glimpses through
Your fairy portals of tenderest blue,
Love's light betraying—beautiful eyes!

Tell-tale eyes, whose lustre soft,
Trembles like those orbs aloft,
Light up my soul with your softest flame,
Evermore changing, yet ever the same;
Light up my pathway, beautiful eyes!

COULD I FORGET!

(SONG.)

AIR—"*Good news from Home.*"

Could I forget! could I forget
The gladsome dreams which once were mine,
My bosom might be happy yet,
And worship find a truer shrine,
And hope with golden lustre shine:
But memory will not, will not sleep,
The wounds have rankled all too deep;
Still time might have some solace yet,
Could I forget! could I forget!

    Could I forget! could I forget
    The anguish of this drear regret,
    Hope's torch might be rekindled yet,
    Could I forget! could I forget!

I deemed the hopes that once I nursed
The rosy flushing of the morn,
It was but the Aurora's light that burst,
And scattered o'er the sky was borne,

A pallid gleam's uncertain track,
Which made the blackness yet more black;
Still joy might light my pathway yet,
Could I forget! could I forget!
  Could I forget! could I forget
  The anguish of this drear regret,
  Hope's torch might be rekindled yet,
  Could I forget! could I forget!

Without a hope, without a fear,
For Fortune's smile or Fortune's frown,
My heart is like the autumn drear,
Its leaves of hope are sere and brown.
But once the sullen winter's through,
Old earth will laugh in verdure new;
So spring might chase my winter yet,
Could I forget! could I forget!
  Could I forget! could I forget
  The anguish of this drear regret,
  Hope's torch might be rekindled yet,
  Could I forget! could I forget!

MY PROPOSED NEW PHILOSOPHY.

" If Thou wilt, let us make three tabernacles; one for Thee, and one for Moses, and one for Elias."

LET us build three tabernacles, and adore
New gods, and walk in a new way;
For those whom I have worshipped heretofore
Have proven vile and faithless—gilded clay.

Uprear the first and lordliest to *Scorn!*
Scorn of the abject worms, that smile and hurt,
Crawling 'twixt heaven and earth, till they be borne
Into congenial darkness—dirt to dirt.

And consecrate the next to *Truth!* though all
Be hollow-hearted, smiling lying smiles,
Plain honest truth but guide us, and I shall
Be disentangled from these circling wiles.

And build the last to *Self!* for I have sought
Too long and vainly others' help to be.
Soul, seek thine own delights, though they be bought
With others' griefs, what ruth have they for thee?

FRAGMENT.

Thus Nature is the ladder whereupon
We mount; and each ascent doth bear us
Nearer and nearer to the Mighty One,
Who, step by step, doth thus prepare us,
Dimly to view His glories.   Naught
By sard-like leap, or bound, or sudden thrust
Is by the mighty mother wrought,
But all in graduation just.
How high may we not rise, if deep and firm our trust !

VALENTINE.

Och ! darlint, 'tisn't civil
  Thus to worry a poor devil:
Sure my heart's in a very bad way;
  It's all with a faver
  Of love for you, you misbelaver,
That I can't get nayther rest night nor day.

  Faith ! I dote upon your beauty,
  From your wreath down to your shoetie:

Don't you beat the other girls all to fits;
  But what's the use of spaking?
  Darlint! sure my heart is breaking—
But you're welcome, Meg Mavourneen, to the bits.

  If things go any further,
  Troth! the upshot will be murther—
You'll be tried and condemned for your charms;
  And 'twould give no repintance,
  If this should be your sintence—
" Imprisonment for life "—in my arms!

THERE IS A STAR.

(SONG.)

There is a star outshining
  All other orbs of night,
And many a fond one pining
  Has blessed its gentle light.
With a serenest splendour
  It greets us from above,
And hopes and memories tender
  Come with the star of love.

THERE IS A STAR.

Like to silver censer,
   By angels hung on high,
Its lustre grows intenser
   The darker grows the sky.
And should the worldling's malice
   Desponding fancies move,
There's a blessing and a solace
   In the gentle star of love.

Sometimes the heavens are shrouded
   From utmost verge to cope,
Sometimes the heart is clouded
   With griefs that see no hope;
But pleasant thoughts returning,
   These darksome fears remove,
And soon again, clear-burning,
   Out shines the star of love.

Our eyes with earnest poring
   To earth are too much given;
Let us, with souls upsoaring,
   Look oftener up to heaven.
And steadiest and clearest
   Of all that shine above,
And brightest still, and dearest,
   Is the silvery star of love.

SONG.

Dark memories in our bosoms
   Lurk deep and will not fly,
As in the fairest blossoms
   The canker poisons lie.
A breath, a word, a trifle,
   Wake thoughts with power to blast,
And vainly would we stifle
   The memory of the past.

MAN.

O MAN! whoe'er thou art, be thou not proud;
What art thou, and what hast thou, that thine heart
With aught should be uplifted?   Doth the crowd
Of nature's workings, cast on every part,
Around, above, into thy being dart
A knowledge of superiority?
Are they so very low that thou shouldst be so high?

Answer when thou art questioned—art thou strong?
Canst thou control old ocean's ordered flow?
Canst thou restrain the wind's most solemn song,
Or quench in night the fire-mount's lurid glow?
Or, when the earthquake groans and writhes below,
Wilt thou ordain it in its course to stay?
And will it list thy words, and will it them obey?

Strength springs from wisdom.   Is thy heart then wise?
Canst thou narrate the origin of things,
Or lure the Iris from the weeping skies?
Is thy mind subtle? can it pierce the springs
Of thought and matter?   With a seraph's wings

Canst thou uprise and probe the mystery
Of the dim future-time? O worm, wilt thou reply?

There is a voice for ever in thy heart,
Urging thee, "Be thou happy;" this the end
All aim at; but their instruments oft thwart
Accomplishment—not more from want of art
Than lack of fitness in themselves innate,
Joined to that earthly sense which makes possession
    sate.

HYMN TO EROS.

Oh thou, who in the earlier days of earth
Wert worshipped as a god, divinest love!
Hear me when I lift up my voice to thee,
And seek thine aid, and pray deliverance
From the fierce storm of thought that makes
My heart sick with an incessant aching.

And shall I bless or curse thee? is the light
Which flushes o'er my soul the roseate dawn,
Of a new day of rapture, or but only
The lurid gleam of a volcano
Heralding on lava-stream of bitterness,

Which will flow darkly o'er my heart, and leave it
Scorched, scarred, and withered, and all desolate,
Herbless, flowerless, when the dew of heaven
Shall fall with its soft healing nevermore?

I have no puling rhyme wherewith to hail
Thine influence; no soft, hurried prayer,
No well-chosen string of sounding sentences;
These I commit to fools who have but dreamed
Of thee and thy divinity; but I,
Who know thee, and am full of thee, whose soul
Is sick and faint, even to agony,
With thy pervading presence—I, with whom
Thou hast been so familiar, day and night,
In waking thoughts and dreams of sleep, all times,
And moods of mind, I call on thee aloud
With a stern voice of passion, for I call
Forth from the vexed abysses of a soul
Warring with doubt, and jealousies, and fears,
Whence a soft tone would be as faintly heard
As 'midst the roar of a strong cataract's torture.

Thou art the soul of earth. Its glens and hills,
Its many waters, and its loud-voiced winds,
Would sleep in death and silence without thee;
'Tis thou who dost endow them with delight.
The beauty of the earth is in the eye,
And not in what it contemplates; and thou

Art light to the dim eyeballs, and thou floatest
Invisibly round all we see, enrobing
The laughing waters, and green fields, and wood-
    lands,
And the star-peopled sky, with loveliness.

All things speak of thee. The soft evening wind,
Laden with stolen fragrance, is thy sigh;
Thy smile makes warm the sunshine, and the song
Of birds is but thy tenderest tones of bliss
Murmured in sleep. But thou delightest most
To harbour in the loved one's face, and laugh
Merrily from her eyes' blue liquid depths,
And frolic in her sunny smile, and gird
Each graceful gesture of her stately form
With a divinest atmosphere of love.

But with the sun there cometh evermore
The shadow, and with thee, O sovran love!
Come jealousy, and doubt, and a strong sense
Of worthlessness. Alas! alas! what hope
Is there to gladden me? if I look up
To the dim sky, there shines not one faint star
To cheer or guide. O foolish heart of mine!
Thou hast no claim in loving, worshipping,
Well nigh adoring her; for all must love her,
And if she smile on thee, doth she not smile
On all? O fool, to dream thou couldst be loved.

Yes, I say this with a true soul. There may
Be one whom she doth love with an affection
That passes infinitely her thought of me,
But there can never be on all the earth,
'Mong all the multitude of men that live,
One who can love her as I love her, for
She is to me, as 'twere, another life,
A second soul; there is but one sweet face
In all the world to me, and that is hers;
She is the sea in which each stream of thought
Is swallowed up and ends. But like a cloud
Doubt hangs upon my heart, and darkens it
With a grim shadow. I wander in the night.
O tyrant love! will the dawn never come?

LIFE AND DEATH.

(A DIRGE.)

Oh river of life! oh river
  That flowest for ever,
    On—ever on.
  No stemming nor breasting
  Thy waves' haughty cresting;
  No pausing, no resting,
    None—no none.

The willows, the sad, sad willows
  Droop over thy billows,
    Until thy stream,
  Scarce seen through their number,
  Looks darksome and sombre,
  And sullen as slumber
    Without a dream.

Oh land of sweet death! oh best land!
  Home of the dead,
  Beyond life's dark billow,
  Beyond grief's dark willow,
  In thee would I pillow
    My aching head.

THE FAREWELL.

Soul of my lute! mine olden friend!
One wailing song—but one—the last!
One backward glance before I rend
The ties that bind me to the past.
Now summer's skies their blue impart,
And summer's blossoms opening swell,
But to the summer of the heart
I bid for aye farewell, farewell.

THE FAREWELL.

Soul of my lute, voiceless so long,
Before thy strings be all unstrung,
Breathe into verse one last sad song,
Though discords stray thy tones among.
The heavy eye is dim with tears,
The bursting heart will throb and swell,
But I can bid to all my fears
And hopes alike farewell, farewell.

Since 'tis so fated be it so;
Strength will not fail me in my need
To bear me up beneath this woe:
And though the heart may wily bleed,
I'll teach my lips a hollow smile,
And mock the thoughts I cannot quell,
And give the world back guile for guile,
And bid old Faith farewell, farewell.

It was my hope, fond, foolish dream,
That love might purchase love again;
I thought that smiles meant what they seem,
And there was one who would not feign.
But Eve a dowry of deceit
Bequeathed her daughters when she fell,
Their smile's a lie, their sighs a cheat;
To smile and sighs farewell, farewell.

DREAMS.

> "We are such stuff
> As dreams are made of, and our little life
> Is rounded with a sleep."—*Tempest*.

Is it asleep or awake that we dream?
Who shall take up the tale and say?
  Truly I know not whether
The visions of night, or the hopes of day,
The thoughts of the dusk, or the thoughts of the gleam,
  Are quickest to fade and wither.

Is it awake or asleep that we dream?
Friendship is tried and proven vain;
  Doubt, and mistrust, and sorrow
Sunder the links of friendship's chain;
Rent ties chase each other in endless stream,
  From weary morrow to morrow.

Is it asleep or awake that we dream?
Is it in love we place our trust?
  What night-dream so deceiving?
Apples of Sodom—ashes and dust—
Youth's Fata Morgana, and age's theme
  Of disenchanted grieving.

Is it awake or asleep that we dream?
Following hope's alluring beck,
    With footstep fast and eager,
We take our path through ruin and wreck
To a dreary waste, at whose bleak extreme
    Dismay and death hold leaguer.

Is it asleep or awake that we dream?
Witness gaiety's votary crowd;
    Witness the mad endeavour,
Ixion-like, to embrace the cloud,
To bask for a while in the accursed beam,
    Then whirl on the wheel for ever.

Is it by day or by night that we dream?
In both—in both—through both there creep
    Shade of sorrows and errors.
To His beloved He giveth sleep;
O gift most worthy the Supreme!
    That sleep unscared by terrors.

THE ENIGMA OF TIME.

JEALOUSLY clutched to thy breast, O Time!
Thou bearest a scroll, as yet unsealed;
When shall the sun-clock index the chime,
That brings the fiat, "Be it revealed?"

THE ENIGMA OF TIME.

Will it be *ever* unsealed, that scroll,
To human eyes, that they see the end?
Will the dreary mystery of life unroll
Ever, that we may comprehend
The awful enigma and secret of time?

Wealth grows greater, and savagedom grows
Greater and greater, day after day;
Almsgiving nursing it, till it knows
A hunger that alms shall never allay.
Daily the hypocrite flourisheth,
Daily the liar and cheat grow rich;
Thus stands the case—no matter what saith
The preacher, mumbling dead words, by which
He would reveal the enigma of time.

Cotton, and iron, and coal, are strong;
Cotton, and iron, and coal—are they wise?
They can whirl the wheel of trade along;
Can they hush the storm of poverty's cries?
Caveat Emptor—so says John Bright;
Caveat Vendor—rather say I.
Perish our trade on left and right,
If it can only build on a lie—
This is *no* secret of thine, O Time!

NELLY.

Laugh out, little Nell, with your grandmother's laugh,
   And the trick of your grandmother's eyes,
Half-waken the dreams of the future, and half
   Of the days that are long gone by;
Toss up in the sunshine your sunshiny curls;
   Oh that the cares of the coming days,
The months of sorrows, the years of perils,
   May be tossed as lightly away.

WRITTEN ON THE DEATH OF MR ROBERT BUCHANAN,

WHO DIED DECEMBER 31, 1875.

Dead—as the year was dying,
   In gusty wind and lashing rain!
He has laid down the weariness of life—
   The fret, and the grief, and the pain.
For many a day, wherein for him
   Lay any charm to make life loved?
The coldness of the shadow grim
   Chilled him and would not be removed.

In truth, with death's companionship
He walked his way these later years,
Until he saw life's hope-stars dip
In darkness all their radiant spheres,
And only faith, afar could see
The star that hangs o'er Calvary.
    Dead—as the year was dying.

THE RIME OF THE WICKED EARL.

NOTE.

An Ayrshire legend supplies the essential outline of this rime. The supernatural element is taken very much as it is found in the old story; but it would not be difficult to accept the facts in their full integrity, and explain them without the aid of any spiritual agency, except so far as there is in every man a spiritual agency, hitherto uncaught in the finest meshes of the metaphysical web—an agency and power apprehended of all, comprehended of none.

PROEM.

In lonely moorland glens grey toothless crones
Mumble out vague and incoherent tales,
In most monotonous, dull undertones,
Reiterated till attention fails.

Broken and caught up like a ravelled thread,
Some scandal of grim lord or lady gay,
Magnified through the mist of years long dead,
Distorted into doubtful disarray.

Laughter and terror going hand in hand,
And retribution bringing up the rear,
Like the lame laggard of a flying band,
That only follows for the following fear.

For we may mark in all these tales antique,
How firm the faith which the narrators hold,
That though despised, and trampled on, and weak,
Under the might of force, or fraud, or gold,

The curse of unjust suffering rises up,
And will not be restrained, but drop by drop
Distils its venomed essence, till the cup
Of retribution brims up to the top.

And that this life which sees the ill deed done,
Sees also the ill end that follows sure;
Impatient thought and vain! That there is One
Who will avenge the friendless and the poor

We know full well; but not the less we know,
That it is *after* death the judgments come,
And that they cannot fail to come; and so
Our querulous impatience should be dumb.

Once on a time I lived among old books,
And heard old stories rhymed o'er day by day,
Reading the part in dim forgotten nooks,
Sequestered from the dusty, hot highway;

Until the quaint old language did become
As a familiar friend, whose aspect rough,
At first cross-grained, and with a touch of gloom;
Morose, forbidding—ay, and somewhat gruff,

Grows lovable on near acquaintanceship,
And soft and sweet beneath the gnarled rind;
And from whose grim, sarcastic, shrivelled lip
Falls consolation, well advised and kind.

So in the telling of this old-world rime,
It may be pardoned me that I did seek
To link some old-world phrases in its chime,
And cast its numbers in a mould antique.

FYTTE THE FIRST.

ARGUMENT.

As the bride delights in the bridegroom, so the old earth delights and evermore will delight in the lusty sun; yea, even till a new choir of the morning stars shall rejoice over the new earth and the new heavens. On a Sabbath in the old killing time, an aged man sat in Rylston Haugh, and read anent the passion of our dear Lord. Earl Sellis of Tralean, being advised of his contumacy, seeks him. The old man wots not of their coming, for his spirit, in waking trance, sees the woful spectacle at the Holy Rood, and the snare is gathered round him. The gladness of life has long since fallen from him, like the greenery from the trees in autumn; and whatsoever of hope remains, points upwards, like a bare fir forest. He curses the earl by that Power who gives to the wind-sower a full harvest; and thereupon falls asleep.

The stars are blanched before the dawn,
    And glimmer cold and white;
And the sky grows pallid with a film
    Of grey and ghostly light,
Until the fiery flush lights up
    Cantyre's bare, ridgy steeps,
And the laverock, from the dew-wet sward,
    To meet the day-god leaps;
Large orbed and red, half vapour-hid,
    He glints the mists with gold,
Yet ever upward surely bends
    To his noonday hold.

It was the noon of the holy day,
    The Sabbath of the Lord,
And an old man sat in a sheltered nook
    And conned the Holy Word.
Only in secret durst he read,
    Only in secret pray,
For the Prelatists sorely vexed the saints
    In that evil day.

It was the noon of the holy day,
    And forth Earl Sellis rode;
And following him in warlike trim,
With reckless bearing, stern and grim,
    Went ritters five abroad.

By ridge and path, through copse and strath,
　　They rode for many a mile;
The grey depths of the earl's cold eye
　　Bright with a cruel smile.
He led them on, nor e'er turned round,
　　Nor spake through all the while:
Across the dreary upland moor
　　Their weary way they made,
On to the edge of a deep ravine,
　　Where further course was stayed.

Their leader sprang from his horse and spake;
　　"We must on foot," quoth he.
They tethered their steeds with the bridle-reins
　　To the fairy's hawthorn tree,
And clambered down the steep glen side,
　　Through hazel-clumps and fern;
With hand and knee they clambered down,
　　Until they reached the burn
That slid o'er the moss, along and across,
　　With many a brawling turn.
Then up the glen, along the stream,
　　With wary steps and slow;
The ravine narrowed to a gorge,
　　And darker it did grow;
It seemed they did, in a few brief strides,
　　From noon to gloaming go.

The old man reads in his lownie nook
    To evite the evil law;
The Book on his knees, and his brow in his hands,
    In the gloom of Rylston Haugh.
His body was there in the dim wood shade,
    Abstracted all and still,
But his soul was with the multitude
That hooting, and jeering, and mocking stood
    On the cursed Judean hill;
Whilst writhing in woful agony,
    Three men on high are raised,
And a few sad women, wailing sore,
    Lie on the ground abased.
To his spirit's ear the scoff and jeer
    Came from old Jewry's crowd,
But in sooth the ear of the body too
    Met a scoff and a jeer as loud:
"Doth the old dotard sleep?" quoth they,
    "Or lies he in a dwam,
Clean doitered with the drowsy lilt
    Of a canting, whiggamore psalm?"

With meaningless stare he eyed the band,
    A moment and no more,
Then closed the Book, and rose to face
    The fate that glared before.
They hauled him forth to an open space:
    Never a word spake he:

Till three stood out with firelocks raised,
    Then he sank down on his knee;
And his prayer rose up to the throne of God
    Like a frost-mist from the sea.
The word was given—the volley fired—
    The echoes of the wood
Awoke at the sound, and each with each
    Did wage a noisy feud.
In the death-throe he writhed—his mouth
    Welled full of the warm blood.
He clutched the grass—he gasped to speak;
    But his mouth was filled with blood.
"And prays he yet?" jeered grim Tralean;
    "His tongue can patter well;
I trow his ben'son will be changed
    To curse with book and bell."

When changed with hate, or woe, or love,
    A power in the heart doth lie,
To give the might of an angel's tongue
    To a mute glance of the eye.
That glance now met Tralean's bold look,
    Clear, calm, and stern, and high,
And graven for aye on Tralean's black heart,
    That glance might never die!

A power seemed to enter the dying man,
    A spirit not of himself,

As when a corse is tenanted
    By some avenging elf.
His right hand up he tossed to heaven,
    From his mouth he spat the blood,
And his solemn eye glared steadily
    At Sellis, where he stood:
"Earth is nigh weary of thy works,
    Of all thou art accursed:
Thy God, thyself, thy fellow-men
    For judgment are athirst.
The blood of the saints whom thou hast slain,
    Cries up from out the dust.
The vintage of wrath is pressed for thee,
    The dregs, and the wine, and the must.
Thine eye hath mocked mine agony,
    'Twill one day be thine own;
In keener pangs thou'lt writhe, and yet
    Thy tongue shall patter none."

Down sank the hand, the eye grew dim,
    And fixed and still the face.
His body to the earth and air—
    His soul to Jesu's grace.

FYTTE THE SECOND.

ARGUMENT.

Three years pass away, three circlings of the appointed seasons, ordained from of old; and Earl Sellis becomes a name muttered in bitterness of heart, and with sore loathing. On a time he was returning to Tralean Castle, when the flushed sun stoops to the west, behind the hills of Cantyre. He falls into a mood of deep musing; but that comes which awakens memory, who hath an easily-broken slumber. A voice pierces the earl's soul, at the which he is mightily moved, and stands a space glamoured; but anon flies, as if fiend-chased, to Tralean Castle, and swoons by reason of his great perturbation.

With garments loose, and hair unbound,
    The Summer danced along;
And tawny Autumn followed straight
    With a glad harvest-song;
Till Winter drave her forth, and held
    The earth in icy chain.
But the young Spring warred with the gruff old carle,
    And overthrew his reign;
And lured the flowers from the frost-freed ground
    By many a kind device,
And nursed them tenderly: and thus
    The seasons circled thrice.
Three years rolled on, and Sellis' name
    Was cursèd everywhere:

The husband, sire, and widow's moan
    Oft woke in sore despair.
But bide the time! such cries as these
    Are wasted not in air.

At early dawn he hied him forth
    On some ungodly quest,
And ere he homeward turned his rein,
    The sun lay in the west.
With foam-flecked chest and reeking flank,
    The gallant steed stretched on,
Now dim in the wood's fast-waning shade,
    In the red gleam bathed anon.
In deepest thought Earl Sellis rode,
    Nor ever looked around.
With sudden shock he woke—his steed
    Had stumbled o'er a mound.
Quick he reined up, and wistly gazed
    Eftsoons to left and right;
And a scene that memory did not love
    Affronted there his sight.
No lettered stone on the little mound
    Betold who slept below.
And wherefore should Earl Sellis start?
    Why shiver coldly so?
A hoarhaired man had perished there
    Upon a summer day,

And the memory of his latest glance
    Had never passed away.

And lo! a voice brake forth, and spake—
    It held the earl in chain—
"Must blood cry up to Abel's God
    For ever, and in vain?
The truth of him who cursed thee here
    Shall sternly proven be.
Naught now remains to thee but this,
    Thy well-won weird to dree."
Whether it was a sprite of God
    Who spoke these words of dole,
Or the evil power who tempted him,
    Or the voice of his own soul,
It is not surely mine to wist;
    But with bitter agony
It moved his mind, as a fierce north wind
    Tosses a lonely tree.

As one upon a rock who hangs
    Over a rushing lynn,
And, 'midst the dizziness of brain
    Wrought by the whirl and din,
Doth feel an impulse keen to leap
    The seething waters in;
And so he trembles as he lies
    Upon the rocky shelf;

But up he springs, with shuddering filled,
    And flies, even from himself,
With frantic speed, nor ever round
    Doth he his eyeballs cast;
With frantic speed, each footstep's pace
    Still fleeter than the last:
So Sellis stood, so Sellis fled
    From Rylston Wood aghast.

His keen spurs ploughed black Danger's side,
    Nor did his speed abate
Till, with a groan, the steed fell down,
    Ten strides from the castle gate.
The warder warned, the knaves rushed out,
    But they to him did seem
To whirl, and leer, and mock, and grin,
Like goblins round the bed of Sin,
    In a drunk nightmare dream.

Into the olden hall he reeled,
    And haggardly looked round;
The glare of lights, the throng of forms,
    The dull, dead, surging sound
Sent the blood pulsing to his brain;
    And thereupon he swooned.

FYTTE THE THIRD.

ARGUMENT.

His gentle wife, albeit she doth know the aching of love grown cold, tends the earl dutifully. But with returning sense comes returning torment, and he seeks an anodyne in the wine-cup's ecstasy. He sits alone—of mortal companionship is none with him—and the wine-god's inspiration, and the whirl of his own thoughts, give to the eye a strange double sight, till the mind endows with life things inanimate. But the solacing cup bears him up with a strong hardihood; and the old witch Lilis comes with her charmed goblet. (She was the first wife of Adam, and by her were the evil angels begotten, as witness the ancient Talmudists.) And the seven deadly sins are with her, seemingly each one more beautiful than the idol of the soul's first love-dream, to whom the worshipping spirit has given all fair gifts and richest fancy treasures, that the shrine may be worthy of the adorer; yet is Lilis more beautiful than they. And the compelling power of the accursed verse is upon him. He drinks, and the end comes on.

> She had a sweet and winsome face,
>   Pale Lady of Tralean,
> And soft and sad as Phœbe's beam
>   The light of her blue een;
> For she had known the agony
>   Of watching, day by day,
> The first fierce tide of her husband's love
>   Ebb, wave by wave, away,
> Till all was gone; and scaith, and scorn,
>   And many an insult deep,
> Became her lot, and sighs and tears
>   Her lullaby to sleep.

Yet aye she sought in deed and thought
   Her wifely part to keep.
And now he lay upon a couch,
   The knaves were all withdrawn,
She tended till the trembling breath
   Came softly like the dawn.
So he did wake; and memory came
   Again to torture him,
To din the curse into his ears,
   And daze his eyeballs dim,
Till round about, in reel and rout,
   All things did seem to swim;
And he was maddened, and did leap
   With grim oath hurriedly to his feet,
Striking aside her who had watched
   With ministry so sweet,
And bade the pantler furnish forth
   Good store of choicest wine,
That Bacchus might dispel the power
   Of the evil sign.

In every sconce a cresset blazed,
   And all alone sat he.
Alone! alone with his gnawing thoughts
Wound round his heart, like grasping knots
   Of hissing snakes—woe's me!
Seven devils from the lowest pit
   Were blanden company.

The wine-god is a freakish god;
   And 'tis his frequent whim
To play strange pranks with the phantasy
   Of those who worship him.
He giveth it a shaping power
   On the brain strange sights to limn;
No limner e'er had shaping power
   Might be compared with him.

'Tis writ of a knight, who dantonless,
   A demon-steed bestrode,
And straight forgot the rhymèd spell
   That ruled the fiend he rode;
So his limbs were rent by the thing hell-sent
   And scattered all abroad.
Thus with the earl: he lost the rein
   O'er his own imagining;
The quaint-carved corbels on the walls
   Seemed leers at him to fling.
With every tassie of the wine
   The more they grinned and leered,
And he laughed and quaffed; for the wine-god made
   His votary non-afeared.
The old Traleans that hung inlimned
   On the panels of Ayrshire oak,
He saw them start from their frames, as if
   By necromancy woke,

And beckoning stand, with mail-gloved hand,
    Then dimly fade away—
He laughed aloud at the ghostly crowd,
    As they did fade away;
And the startled walls in echo back
    Will nothing him dismay.
And straight a troop of forms sprang up,
And one did bear a gem-decked cup,
    Seemed full of ruby-flame.
None ever was so fair as she,
None ever had such witchery,
    And Lilis is her name.

'Tis she who sits by the lone sea-brink,
    Unwary men to entice,
By the spell that lies in her woven hair,
And her luring smile, beyond compare,
And her snatches of song, antique and rare,
    And her wonderful flashing eyes.
Wreathing around her a charmèd dance,
    Breathing a charmèd song,
A choir of seven sister-elves
    Usher her along.
With flashing arms, and floating hair,
    And swimming eyes of love,
To the measure of the cadenced song
    Their glancing footsteps move;

But they, like stars when the moon is up,
Paled before her of the flameful cup—
   Nor might a contrast prove.
Up to the earl in mazy whirl
   The spirit sisters glide;
With motions warm, and free, and bland,
Like dancing girls of Paynim land,
And he gazes on the twining band,
   Flush-faced and eager-eyed.
She who doth bear the goblet rare
   Smiles graciously on him,
And the wondrous sheen of her lustrous een
   Maketh the lamps burn dim.
Nearer the earl with every whirl
   The seven and the one glide on.
Their charmèd chant now urgeth him
To drink from the glamoured goblet's brim
   The wine that ruby shone:
And that pleasure was his, and perfect bliss,
When his lips the goblet's brink should kiss;
   And sorrow be no more known.

The Witch-Song.

LUST.

"Keen the delight of love!
   When lips meet lips,

And the glowing eyes above
   Have a moment's eclipse;
When heart pants to heart
   With a trembling desire,
And each glance is a dart
   Winged with passionate fire."

ANGER.

"Keen the delight of war!
   The stern joy of battle,
When near and afar
   Sounds the sky-cleaving rattle;
When face glares into face,
   With knit brows and hard breath,
And the drunken heart reels
   With the red wine of death!
And the strong reaper, Mars,
   Stalks his harvest-field thorough,
Gathering his ripe sheaves
   From furrow to furrow."

HATE.

"Keen the delight of revenge!
   Which, like a sleuth-hound,
Will tire not, nor range,
   Till it close with a bound.

From the start to the capture
    The hot hate grows stronger,
Till it drink in with rapture
    The throes of the wronger."

INTEMPERANCE.

"Keen the delight of wine!
    When it beads up and dances,
With a flame more divine
    Than a thousand love-glances;
And like spring through the forest
    It thrills through the veins;
And of anquish the sorest
    What memory remains?"

AVARICE.

"Keen the delight of power!
    And in wealth 'tis uphoarded.
Woo me, and this be the dower—
    O'er the worldlings to lord it,
Gaze on the tawny gold,
    Or the gem's shifting shimmer,
Till the wine-flush looks cold,
    And beauty's sheen dimmer.

The world, now as erst,
    Sweats and racks the brain, thinking
To quench my fierce thirst,
    Which grows fiercer with drinking."

JEALOUSY.

"Oh! the glare of the weary day,
    The gloom of the weary night,
And the heart that eats itself away,
    And of dolour makes delight.
And the sting of the sleepless snake,
    Nestled in the breast;
Waking to shudder, sleeping to ache,
    Never to rest!"

PRIDE.

"My sisters move with aiding arms
    That interlace and meet!
I move along; my stronger charms
    Are in themselves complete."

SLOTH.

"Keener than all the delight
    Of deep, deep rest!
Which falls like the night
    With its dews on the breast.

> Even as to the broad ocean
> All water-streams tend,
> So each work and emotion
> Here hath its end!"

LILIS.

> "Dark of soul! such as we love—
> With a curse upon thee—as on us—
> We have ever been with thee—unseen but near—
> Till the charm was wrought, whereby we appear
> Visibly to thee—now—and thus.
> Drink and prove
> That in the sphere of our chalice here
> Is treasured up, by an alchemy rarest,
> Each delight thou holdest most dear,
> And a balm for every ill thou bearest!
> The dew of a thousand kisses,
> The soul of a thousand sighs,
> The thrill of a thousand blisses,
> The lust of a thousand eyes,
> Are as naught—yea, less than naught,
> To the Elysium that lies
> In this wine: and my cup is overfraught."

I cannot tell how sweet their song:
It had compelling power and strong,

Like every song of sin.
And as one drinks the sunshine clear
Who long hath pined in duress drear,
   Earl Sellis drank it in.
He drank it in, and it did sway
   His soul with subtle craft:
He clutched the cup, he tossed it up,
   And sought an eager draught.

He had not held the flaming wine
   A moment to his lips,
Ere the bright form vanished from his view,
And the lamps did burn a ghastly blue,
And all things wore an eerie hue,
   As in a sun eclipse:
And sounds there were came wandering by,
The sound as of one long, wailing sigh,
   Anon a burst of laughter;
Which echoed along, each time more strong,
   More bitter far, and dafter;
He well might ken no mortal men
   E'er laughed that eldrich laughter.
His veins did each like pulses beat,
   His heart was stricken cold,
He sought to stand, but straight fell down
To the floor, with never a sigh or groan,
   Ere two could well be told.

FYTTE THE FOURTH.

ARGUMENT.

Through the terror of the long night sits Lady Tralean, and for very fear her tiring-woman is with her. The day comes, and they are loosened from the chain of the night-terror. And the same fear is upon the menials. Consciousness comes again to the earl, and the full weight of the curse presses him sorely for seven days, which is an eternity; and on the seventh, when the sun leaves the earth to the slumbers of the night-time, and to the vigils of the sleepless stars, and the sad moon (who is wan with sorrow at the rushing song of the fiery planets, which she may in no wise answer—being less noble than they), with fierce convulsions the agony of life forsaketh him, and the curse in this mid-world hath its consummation.

 Bitter of heart, in her sad bower
 She sat through all the weird night hour,
  Sad Lady of Tralean!
 And with her sat her tiring-lass,
 And their hearts drink in, as the weary hours pass,
  Strange awe, and dread, and teen.
 Half-woke, half-tranced in nightmare's grip
  They sat, till came the day,
 Like healing dew it fell on them,
  They twain began to pray;
 Then the bonds of the thing that seemed so strong
  Were weak as gossamer:
 All foul things fly when God's dear light
  Is given to appear.

The varlets flocked all to the common hall,
    Each looked in his neighbour's eyes,
If his own fear did there appear,
    And his own surprise;
And spake in whispers, each to each
    Of the strange sound yestreen.
Slow passed the hour, till from the bower
    Came the pale Lady of Tralean;
And two went with her to the hall,
    And there Earl Sellis lay,
As stiff and still, as cold and chill,
    As life had fled for aye.

But he woke again to agony,
    And the work of the curse returned,
His eyes, like balls of molten lead,
    Within their sockets burned,
His tongue was withered, and powerless all
    To speak his torments deep,
And the burning thirst, and the gnawing woe:
Never again might Earl Sellis know
    The blessing of sweet sleep.
Thus, wrapped about with tortures keen
As with a robe, lived Earl Tralean
    While seven long days did roll,
With never a voice wherewith to noise
    The anguish of his soul.

The close of the seventh day drew on:
    He stood on a turret high,
And looked around to the laughing ground,
    To the sea, and the quiet sky.
The sun was smiling his parting smile,
    The glad earth drank it in:

Faint in the east the filmy moon
    Hung flecked, and horned, and thin;
And Hesperus alone was seen,
The silver page of the silver queen;
And the winds were moving through the trees
    With a low, lulling din:
O God! so beautiful without,
    So terrible within!

Like the great God who tendeth all,
    And by Whom all have been,
The sun shone ruddily on each—
On the leaping wave that lit the beach
    With a fantastic sheen,
On tree, on rock, on mead, on cloud,
    And eke on Earl Tralean.
Alike on all the red sun shone,
    Never a spot was dim;
And all were glad, save the cursèd man—
    The quiet was a hell to him.

To his reinless fancy the parting sun
    A glaring aspect had,
And winds, and waters, and rustling leaves
    Strange tongues to hiss him mad.
As a man might seize an unweaned child
    And press its breath away,
A strong convulsion seized the earl:
    Then sank the orb of day:
It shook his limbs, it griped his heart,
With straining grip in every part,
    Till life had passed away!

Three days in pall the body lay,
    His widowed dame kept weeping,
And on the fourth the mourners came
To lay him with those of the Sellis name,
    In the kirk vault sleeping.

FYTTE THE FIFTH.

ARGUMENT.

Each Wind hath its own Spirit, and the West Wind hath a gentle Spirit—but over all rules the GREAT ONE, who has appointed laws for their governance, and sure bounds which they may not transgress, though they be freer and more restless than any other of the creatures of the Eternal Lord. For three days the Winds had been lulled in deep quietude, but on the fourth the fell East Wind flew out and battled with the night-gathered clouds, till the rain was lashed down, and the lightning in a ceaseless shower. And five seafaring men who were caught in the overtaking fury of the tempest, witness a selcouth ferlie —even a ship of fire—which steers straight, against wind and tide, to the Carrick coast, crossing, in its course, the forefoot of the fishers' craft. One has the hardihood to challenge it. The response.

Three days the winds were tranquil,
    Still as the soul of that star
That follows the sun, and flies the sun,
    Now near, and now afar.
Then the angry sprite of the strong East Wind
    Rushed out in his stormy car,
With his blasts all marshalled in array,
    As a chief goes forth to war;
And the Spirit who dwells in the wandering cloud
    That changes as it drifts,
Who maketh his throne on the highest zone
    Of his vapour-clifts,
Was all discomfited thereat,
    And showered down tears of rain,
Big, bitter drops of angry grief,
    And westward drave amain.
Each cloud was cloven, and from the cleft
    The leaming fire-balls leapt;
No pause between each fireshower keen,
    The thunders never slept.

As a hawk swoops down upon a dove,
    Even so the tempest smote
With madd'ning wind and maddened wave,
    A hapless fishing boat.
Each plank was shook, each rope was strained,
    All hope had fled each breast,
They saw in the gloom a strange thing come
    Sailing from the west.

Its shape was a ship's—but, gramercy!
    It seemèd all aflame,*
'Gainst wind and sea, with headlong speed,
    Due east, the strange thing came.
Aghast they stared as it drave on;
    A ship, and all of fire,
Nor did it seem to burn away,
    But drew on nigh and nigher.
Five men were in the fishing craft,
    And four were choked with fears,
Though they had sailed upon the sea
Almost since they had left the knee,
    Well on to forty years.

---

* The phenomenon of a fiery meteor has been occasionally seen on the Carrick coast. It is of interest in so far as it may be a matter of speculation whether the (supposed) signal which induced Robert the Bruce to quit Arran and cross over to Turnberry Castle, may not have been of this nature.—See "Lord of the Isles," canto v, st. 17, and Mr Joseph Train's note thereon.

The timoneer was a hardy wight,
    Nor wife nor bairns had he,
Nor cared he aught for godly things,
    Or godly companie;
And stoutly he did parley this
    Strange wanderer on the sea,
"Whence comes the ship, and whither bound?"—
    His shipmates shut their een—
A shriek of laughter burst—"From Hell!
    To the burial of Tralean!"
Straight on it sped, and colourèd
    The vext wave in its flying
With changing tint, like those that glint
    The back o' the dolphin dying;
Straight on it steered, nor tacked, nor veered,
Till to the Cove Tralean it neared,
    Then vanished from their eying.

FYTTE THE SIXTH.

ARGUMENT.

Earl Sellis is an old name in the countryside, so that there be many to follow the corse, notwithstanding the overcoming might of the storm and the strange wind that ever withstands their progress onward. In all living creatures the lesser fear is swallowed up of the greater, and birds of alien and diverse natures companion together, even on the hearse, till the bird of ill omen displaces them; whereupon the bier is arrested on

Strumnock Brig; for no charm, though of the strongest, may avail further than the midst of a running stream. Verily, prayer is the true ladder of Jacob, whereupon angels go up and down, and it is seen to be so by every one whose head is brought low, and pillowed on the hard stone; and through it comes all deliverance.

In Tralean Hall the mourners all
   (As in a bygone verse
I told) were met: all things prepared,
Forth from the castle gate they fared,
   The dead earl in his hearse.
The noon might well be matched with night;
   Meanwhile, with furious dunt,
A roaring wind did buffet them
   And ever seemed in front;
Wend as they might that roaring wind
   Was ever in their front.

It felled down trees athwart their path,
   No birds might perch on sprays,
But on the wings of that strong wind
   Were hurtled divers ways.
And some dazed blind by those keen fires
   The air was filled withal,
Lost fear of man in mightier fear,
   And perched upon the pall,
In midst of that great train of men,
Though wont on moor, or beach, or glen,
   To fly the urchin's "tshew!"

Together cowered the cushet dove,
    The kite, and shy seamew,
With blackbird, pyet, throssel, rook,
    Erst never seen in crew.

Till with a dismal clang of wings
    There swooped a raven down
Upon the bier—but ere he lit,
    Each other bird had flown.
It hath, I wist, in ages all
    Been bird of omen ill,
And now upon old Strumnock Brig
    The earl's hearse stood still!
Six big-boned Flanders mares were yoked
    But naught could they prevail,
Against the charm that held them there
    Their strength might not avail,
Nor voice, nor scourge, nor spur could urge
    Them forward for a thraw;
The hearse stood still, all hearts were chill
    With an eerie sense of awe.
Mad with the force of many burns,
    In current fierce and heady,
The Strumnock raved and roared amain;
As 'twere a snake in mortal pain,
It writhed and coiled, it seethed and boiled
    In many a hoary eddy.

In all that train of frozen men
    But one had voice to pray,
'Twas he who read the Holy Word
    Upon the Sabbath Day.
"O God! when Thy fierce jealousy
    Is kindled into wrath,
We are as worms beneath Thy feet,
    As stubble in Thy path;
Our hearts melt in us, with strong fear
    Our very souls decay,
Where is our strength, or who our help,
    If Thou be not our stay?
And oh! if in Thy justest wrath
    To save Thou dost deny;
Give us but light, Thy blessed light!
    Give us but light to die!
Turn not Thy face away from us,
    Thou God who rul'st on high!"

Thereat a burst of levin-light
    Girt heaven as with a zone;
As 'twere the welkin cloven in twain,
And there came streaming down amain
    The light that hides the throne.
Blind for a space the mourners stood,
And when again the hearse they viewed,
    The evil bird had flown.

Then, like a sapling pinned to earth,
  When loosened from the strain,
With eager start leapt every heart
  Back to its place again.
Nor scourge nor spur could urge or stir
  The steeds, until His name
Was uttered by the holy man,
  In thunder and in flame.
But now they started with their load,
  And it was easy work,
Easily, easily haled they it
  On to the village kirk.
They laid him in the Sellis vault,
  The vault beside the porch,
With the thunder for a coronach,
  The lightning for a torch!

FYTTE THE SEVENTH.

ARGUMENT.

Very solacing are the words of the wise man, "There is a time to die." Yea! the weariness of life endures not for evermore, for unto all is appointed a rest and a soft slumber after the heat and burden of the day; and as each worker has stoutly and faithfully filled up his apportioned time, so it is the more welcome, and comes upon him with a high music, in its very stillness more to be desired than the concord of many harpers harping cunningly on their harps.

All still he lies in that dank vault,
   And ever still hath lain,
Still, calm, and still! though minstrel play
Death's song in many a divers way:
Still, calm, and still! this ever will
   Be burden of the strain.

The kirk around, in the churchyard ground
   Lie buried many folk,
And their silence speechful is, as if
   A trump-tongued angel spoke;
And is it not, in sooth, a voice
   That Azrael hath spoke?
And oft I walk in the kirkyard
   At the pleasant hour of noon,
When there's not a cloud to fleck the breadth
   Of the azure sky of June:
And oftentimes I walk therein
   Beneath the bending moon,
And when I walk therein, my soul
   Saith with a yearning sigh,
"Both one and all, or great or small,
   How peacefully they lie!"

Under the golden sunshine,
   In the happy summer-time,
And on the raw-cold winter morn,
   Under the silver rime:

Or cold or warm, in calm or storm,
    They ne'er are stirred or started;
How silently and still they lie,
    All these old departed!

And oft I think, what time my brain
    Is full of old-world fancies,
Surely this many-aiming world
    Is but a hall of dances.
After the gillie-callum,
    After the blythe strathspey,
After the circle-dance, or reel,
    All hasten the same way;
After the quick-tript morrice,
    After the stately pavan,
They take their fill of welcome rest
    In this quiet haven.

Or slow or swift the pace or shift,
    The changing and the doubling,
Their dancing done, all lie at one,
    Untroubled, and untroubling.
He who oppressed, and they who bore,
    All calmly lie together,
And, fardel-freed, nor note nor heed
    The rain or sunny weather.

RIME OF THE WICKED EARL.

As one who bravely lived and died,
    Large-hearted Raleigh, has it,
Pride's pomp, scorn's scoff, hate's self-torment,
    Joy's smile, Faith's carriage placid,
All hid and sepulchred beneath
    These twain dead words, "*Hic jacet.*"*

O Fancy! who hast woven my strain,
    Be thy glance homeward slanted;
O Soul! thy yearning after quiet
    Will not be ever thwarted:
Be calm in hope. How still they lie,
    All these old departed!

---

* "O eloquent, just, and mighty Death! whom none could advise, thou hast persuaded; what none hath dared, thou hast done; and whom all the world hath flattered, thou only hast cast out of the world and despised; thou hast drawn together all the far-stretched greatness, all the pride, cruelty, and ambition of man, and covered all over with these two narrow words, *Hic Jacet.*"—Sir Walter Raleigh, "History of the World."

INDEX OF FIRST LINES.

	PAGE
Aching heart, what wouldst thou more now?	72
After a faithful priesthood—long confessed,	81
All noon I loitered in the sheltering wood,	2
Although we seek in sunny eyes,	109
And you're back to Bankier,	28
Beautiful eyes, that swim and dance,	121
Be still! be still! though thou shouldst break,	36
Closer and nearer still, Annie! closer and nearer still,	16
Could I forget! could I forget,	122
Could the heart, when hope has perished,	37
Dark memories in our bosoms,	128
Dark memories of the captive and betrayed,	73
Dead—as the year was dying,	139
Doon by whare rashy Bonny rins,	114
Evening's shades, as daylight fades,	1
From the Valhalla—from Gladsheim he passed,	67
Here's the prattle of the burn,	89
I looked on a fountain,	33
In lonely moorland glens grey toothless crones,	141
In the reign of the Magnificent,	92
In the solemn depths of the still night skies,	38

INDEX OF FIRST LINES.

	PAGE
In youth's happy El Dorado,	55
Is it asleep or awake we dream?	136
Jealously clutched to thy breast, O Time,	137
Laugh out, little Nell, with your grandmother's laugh,	139
Let us build three tabernacles, and adore,	124
Little Nelly—chattering Nelly,	78
Lonely sitting—lonely sitting,	41
Many a time, ay, many a time, and oft,	118
Mingling soft memories of years fled for aye,	44
Mirror thyself in the wave, O Star,	80
Miss Shaw was wed on Hogmanay,	34
O breeze of the autumn woods,	88
O man! whoe'er thou art, be thou not proud,	129
Och! darlint, 'tisn't civil,	125
Oh river of life! oh river,	133
Oh thou, who in the earlier days of earth,	130
On the threshold of the year,	50
Seize, oh seize with nimble fingers,	117
Soul of my lute! mine olden friend,	134
The harvest-time is past, and the ripe sheaves,	39
The memories o' the aulden days,	111
The song itself is nothing :—but the name,	5
The summer snow lay thick upon the hedges,	52
There are two sides to every picture,	64
There is a star outshining,	126
There only are two things on which the eye,	117
They deave me wi' clavers,	110
Though faint and vigour-wasted from the loss,	57
Though the rolling of rivers,	85
Threescore and ten, and then he passed from us,	84
Thus Nature is the ladder whereupon,	125
Trudging along, my stick and I,	12

INDEX OF FIRST LINES.

	PAGE
Under the beeches of Earlswood Chase,	62
Was he not wise, that ancient sage,	119
Weary, weary of the sunlight,	75
We bind ourselves to life with wreaths of flowers,	82
What a pettish little fairy,	108
When the wheat was as high as my daughter's head,	65
Why should I waste my heart on one,	31
Winter comes, and winds are wandering,	116
Woe follows even when the reaper Death,	79
Yes! deck her out in her bridal robes,	39
You came with the sunshine,	115

www.ingramcontent.com/pod-product-compliance
Lightning Source LLC
Chambersburg PA
CBHW020829190426
43197CB00037B/738